JERÓNIMOS ABBEY OF SANTA MARIA

JERÓNIMOS ABBEY OF SANTA MARIA

PAULO PEREIRA

SCALA

Ministério da Cultura

INSTITUTO
PORTUGUÊS DO
PATRIMÓNIO
ARQUITECTÓNICO

© Instituto Português do Património Arquitectónico (IPPAR)
and Scala Publishers, 2002

First published in 2002 by Scala Publishers Ltd
Gloucester Mansions
140a Shaftesbury Avenue
London WC2H 8HD

Designed by Andrew Shoolbred
Translated from the Portuguese by Isabel Varea for
Ros Schwartz Translations
Edited by Ros Schwartz

Printed in Spain by Gráficas Santamaría S.A.

ISBN 1 85759 179 8

Photographic credits
All photographs by Luis Pavão, except those on pages 14, 15, 16, 17, 18, 50, 52

Plans © IPPAR

We wish to thank:
All the organizations that gave permission for the use of pictures for this book,
Alexandra Frexes, and Dulce de Freitas Ferraz (IPPAR), for organizing the pho-
tography and helping with editorial content; the photographer Luis Pavão for
his tenacity and instinctive understanding of this project (and others).

Thanks to the following for their cooperation:
Mosteiro dos Jerónimos (IPPAR)
Departamento de Coordenação dos Serviços Dependentes/ Department for
the Coordination of Subsidiary Services (IPPAR)

Abbreviations:
AN/TT (Arquivos Nacionais/National Archives, Torre do Tombo)
BNL (Bibiloteca Nacional/National Library, Lisbon)
MC (Museu da Cidade, Câmara Municipal, Lisboa/Lisbon Municipal Museum)
IPM (Instituto Português de Museus/Portuguese Museum Institute)

CONTENTS

Cloister: detail of
central pillar of window
arch

FOREWORD

The Monastery of Santa Maria de Belém is one of Portugal's best-known monuments. At the height of the Romantic period, it became the starting point on the slow and steady path towards recognition of what we have come to know as 'heritage ideology'. As a national symbol, the monastery attracted the attention of countless art and architectural historians, appearing in specialist publications even before the mid-nineteenth century. Later, the monument was included in the itinerary of every visitor to Lisbon, confirming its status as an exceptional building in the context of an already long-established tourist culture.

The year 2001 marked the 500th anniversary of the monastery's foundation. This symbolic date was suitably celebrated with a combination of special events, publicity campaigns and a programme of research, based on the knowledge available to us at the start of the new millennium. As a result, the Mosteiro dos Jerónimos has achieved an even higher profile, to which this book will certainly contribute.

The Mosteiro dos Jerónimos is not simply a monument to Portuguese discoveries, which include, as some chroniclers claimed, Vasco da Gama's discovery of the sea route to India. It is also a monument to art and architecture from the period c.1500–50. Here we find the most spectacular expression of the Portuguese version of the late Gothic style, which art historians have felicitously named 'Manueline style' in tribute to the monastery's founder, King Manuel I (who reigned 1495 – 1521), combined with elegant Classicism and Counter-Reformation influences.

The building contains so many things, one of the most striking and important of which is its astonishing imperial symbolism intimately bound up with a vision of the worldwide spread of Christianity.

An intricate but exceptionally beautiful interweaving of forms and ideas has made the Jerónimos one of the world's most famous monuments, which deservedly became a World Heritage Site in 1983. We now invite the reader to discover – or perhaps rediscover – the monastery.

Luis Ferreira Calado
(President of IPPAR, the Portuguese Institute for Architectural Heritage)

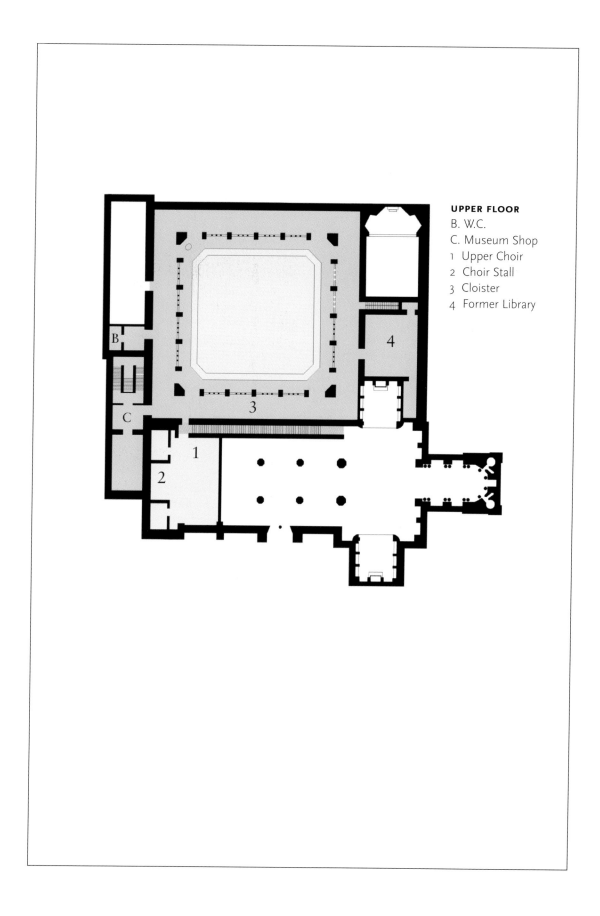

UPPER FLOOR
B. W.C.
C. Museum Shop
1 Upper Choir
2 Choir Stall
3 Cloister
4 Former Library

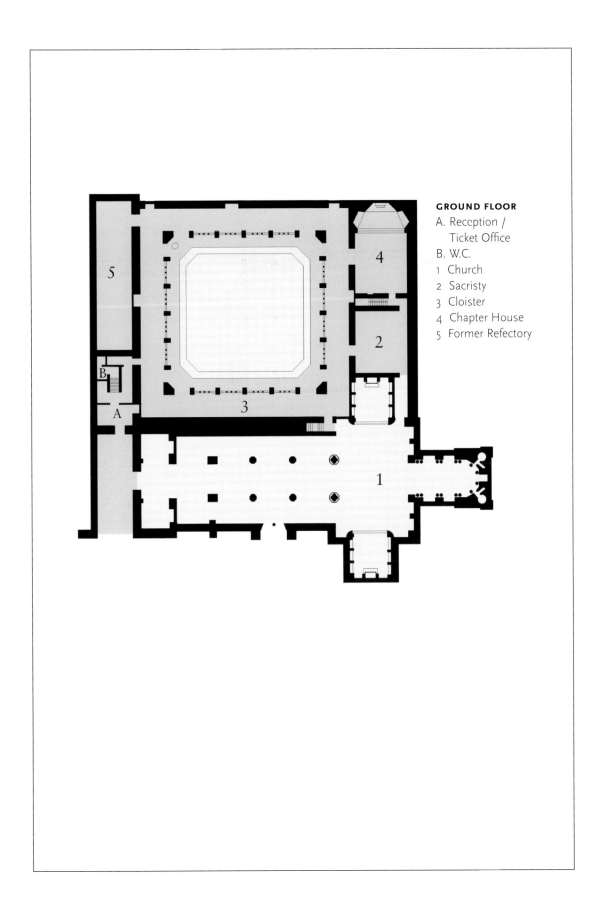

GROUND FLOOR

A. Reception /
   Ticket Office
B. W.C.
1 Church
2 Sacristy
3 Cloister
4 Chapter House
5 Former Refectory

Sculpted group on
the buttress of the
South Portal, with
the Prophets in the
foreground

THE FOUNDATION OF THE MONASTERY

FROM RESTELO TO BELÉM

In the Middle Ages, Restelo, now part of the parish of Belém, was a small coastal village on the eastern outskirts of Lisbon, where ships could be anchored while their crews came ashore. As Restelo became an increasingly important seaport, a chapel was founded in honour of Our Lady, Star of the Sea, traditionally the seafarers' protector and guide. It may be that the name of the place was linked with that of the chapel's patron saint and that *rastrelo* or *restrelo* was a corruption of *estrela* (star), but this is uncertain. What is certain is that the chapel and its patron saint had maritime associations. The name was also an allusion to the story of the Three Wise Men who were guided to the Infant Jesus in Bethlehem (Belém in Portuguese) by a miraculous star.

Prince Henry the Navigator gave orders for the chapel to be extended and named Santa Maria de Belém, so maintaining the connection with its original patron saint. The new chapel was administered by the military and religious Order of Christ. Its main purpose was to take care of the spiritual needs of sailors. It was, however, only a small building and, by the late fifteenth century, it had fallen into disuse, despite the powerful symbolic value it acquired from its association with Vasco da Gama. It was here that the navigator prayed and kept vigil on the eve of the departure of his fleet on 7 July 1497.

Strictly speaking, the history of the Mosteiro de Santa Maria de Belém only began in 1495, when King Manuel I asked permission of the Holy See to found a monastery for the Jeronimite Order on the site of the former chapel of the Order of Christ.

In 1496, the monarch received a positive response, in the form of a Papal Bull issued by Pope Alexander VI. Plans went ahead against a somewhat unusual political backdrop. In 1498, as heirs presumptive to the throne of Castile and León, King Manuel and Queen Isabel travelled to Spain to receive oaths of allegiance. In the same year, however, the queen became fatally ill and died before returning to Portugal. Nevertheless, it was around this time that Manuel made a donation to the Jeronimite monks of Restelo, granting them one twentieth of the taxes levied on gold from Guinea. After Vasco da Gama's triumphant return from the voyage on which he discovered the sea route to India, the king provided even more funds for the new monastery. The Jeronimites officially took possession of the site on 21 April 1500. Meanwhile, following the death of his eldest son Prince Miguel, the monarch married for a second time. He chose as his bride Queen Isabel's sister, María of Castile, a diplomatic move which served his interest in keeping alive his claims to the throne of Castile and so achieve the longed-for unification with Spain under the crown of Portugal. His protection and patronage of the Jeronimite Order may also have been politically motivated, since, in the words of the Portuguese historian Rafael Moreira, it was 'a Spanish order whose vocation was to perpetuate the funerary cult of the ruling dynasty of Castile'.

In 1501 or 1502 (the year is uncertain), on 6 January – the feast of the Epiphany – the foundation stone of the new monastery was laid. In 1503 the Jeronimite monks received a further contribution

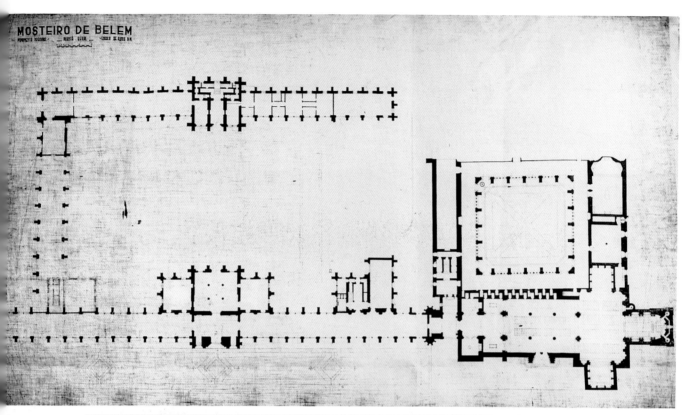

MOSTEIRO DE BELEM

(Previous page) View of the Mosteiro dos Jerónimos, south façade

(Above) Plan of the Mosteiro dos Jerónimos

Mosteiro dos Jerónimos, oil on canvas, by Filipe Lobo (National Museum of Ancient Art)

(Opposite) Aerial view of the Mosteiro dos Jerónimos

of one twentieth of the taxes levied on goods imported from India, which represented the biggest injection of funds ever received by the order.

At this point, legend and history become intertwined. According to the chroniclers, the monastery was built as an act of thanksgiving for the discovery of the sea route to India. This version is doubtful from an historical point of view, since the monastery was founded in 1495, three years before that momentous event. Nevertheless, it would be wrong to dismiss the legendary link between the Jeronimite house and the commemoration of Vasco da Gama's voyage of discovery. The relative short space of time between the king's decision to found a religious house at this location and his subsequent, increasingly generous, donations recorded after Vasco da Gama's return from his first expedition, and his even more lavish contributions after his second, underline the connection between the Mosteiro de Santa Maria de Belém and revenue from Indian trade. At the same time, it was obviously intended as a tangible expression of the ideology of enterprise, an ideology pursued in Portugal with almost religious fervour.

It is significant that the first stone was laid on the feast of Epiphany – the day commemorating the coming of the Three Kings, who travelled from far away to offer the Christ Child the riches of their native lands, in an act which symbolized universal homage to the new-born Messiah. It is also significant that the choice of saint to whom the monastery was dedicated (inherited from Henry the Navigator but imbued with deeper, mythical meaning by King Manuel) was an apparent attempt to transform Restelo into a new Bethlehem, a new Crib and a new point of departure for Christianity. The whole concept is in keeping with the messianic spirit of the Manueline era, represented, as we shall see, in the symbolic nature of the monastery's ornamentation. The unification of Christians scattered across the world, the celebrated search for the empire of the mythical

Eastern monarch and priest, Prester John (which continued during the reign and under the patronage of Manuel I), and even the miracles and 'portents' of the period, magically associated with the advent of the second half of the millennium, are all factors to be taken into account when considering the symbolism of the monastery at Belém.

The historian João de Barros called Belém 'the door through which all the triumphs of the conquest of the Orient might enter'. As a tribute to Vasco da Gama, King Manuel ordered the construction of '26 niches' devoted to discoveries and conquests in India. According to the specification drawn up in 1510 by the king's secretary António Carneiro, the niches were to contain very precise iconographic and narrative references to the ships of Restelo 'which put to sea with the Cross of Christ on their sails . . . borne by angels, with the name of each vessel on the side'. They would also refer to the passage around the Cape of Good Hope and the arrivals in or conquests of Sofala, Mozambique, Quiloa, Mombassa, Brava, Socotra, Cochin, Calicut, Cananor, Taprobana and Chaul. All of this suggests the degree of care and preparation that went into the decoration of the monastery. Equally detailed instruction would have been drawn up for the two additional niches, which are unfortunately not documented.

Hence, the actual date of the construction of the monastery – after Vasco da Gama's return to Portugal – confirms its intended purpose as a celebration of imperial glory. Historians writing in the mid-sixteenth century have very little to say about this objective and many tend to romanticize the facts. In 1501 or 1502 King Manuel had no thought of erecting a small, unassuming hermitage. He wanted a powerful piece of propaganda in the shape of a great monastic house.

THE JERONIMITE MONKS

The Order of St Jerome first emerged in Italy in 1377 as a religious movement led by Tommasucio da Duccio, originally a member of the Franciscan Third Order. It was a closed order, devoted to prayer, contemplation and study, with distinct reformist leanings. Withdrawing from the world in obedience to the precepts of their founder, the Jeronimite monks tried to emulate the life of St Jerome, a desert hermit and an important – possibly *the* most important – Christian intellectual. In the early days of the Church, St Jerome helped to shape the definitive form of the scriptural texts,

The Mosteiro in the late 18th century, engraving by L'Eveque. We can see that the monastery was still close to the seashore and observe the movement of the boats, most of them engaged in small-scale commerce. The church has the original bell-tower, while the dormitory block extends westwards in the 16th-century configuration, with irregular roofs and façades, the lower arches boarded up and windows haphazardly placed. The Torre de Belém is seen in the background on the river bank, with the Forte da Praia (the ancient fort) on the site of the present Belém Cultural Centre

(Opposite) *Mosteiro dos Jerónimos,* pre-1868 watercolour (National Museum of Ancient Art), very clearly showing the Sala dos Reis (Hall of the Kings) and the porch

revising the Latin translation of the New Testament and translating the Old Testament from Greek to Latin between AD 382 and 405.

The Jeronimites arrived in Portugal in the fourteenth century, but it was in the fifteenth, during the reign of Afonso V, that the order became widely recognized and respected as a significant, autonomous organization. The monks established their headquarters at the little monastery of Penha Longa, built in 1448. The Portuguese court had a high regard for the Jeronimites and that tradition of respect was to continue, at least until the reign of King John III.

In the fifteenth century, the Portuguese branch of the Jeronimites enjoyed the same privileges as their brethren in Castile. The latter exercised considerable political and diplomatic influence because of their close ties with the ruling dynasty of Castile. Their mother house was the fabulously wealthy monastery of Santa María de Guadalupe. As the century progressed, the order consolidated its position in Portugal. Not surprisingly, it was encouraged by Manuel, who seems to have been particularly attached to the memory and the political strategy of Afonso V, and less inclined to follow the policies of his predecessor John II. Apart from his obvious devotion to St Jerome, which led to his decision to place a life-like image of the saint over the west door of the monastery, his sympathy with the Jeronimite monks arose from their sense of renewed spirituality, unlike other orders, some of which engaged in disreputable activities.

It was no coincidence that, during the reign of Manuel's successor, the Jeronimites would be the ones to undertake a comprehensive programme of reform of other monastic orders. The Order of Christ was reformed by the Jeronimite monk António de Lisboa; another Jeronimite, Brás de Barros, did the same with the Augustinians and the congregation of Santa Cruz de Coimbra. Even Coimbra University was reorganized, under its Jeronimite rector, Diogo de Murça.

As Felicidade Alves pointed out: 'the Jeronimites [were] a monastic order, focusing primarily on divine worship and its intrinsic splendour, with no direct vocation for evangelical or pastoral activities among the masses. King Manuel apparently preferred to establish a monastery where theology and the beauty of the liturgy were the predominant concerns.' This agenda was well suited to the realities of a world on the threshold of the sixteenth century and the second half of the millennium. The Jeronimites would also have a marked effect on the character of other monastic communities in Portugal. The argument is further supported by the sovereign's declared intention to found

Cloister of the Monastery of Belém, lithograph by William Barclay, from the 19th-century album *Le Portugal Pittoresque et Architectural* (City Museum, Lisbon). The cloister had not yet been restored. The arches on the upper storey are boarded up and without tracery. In the centre of the cloister is a rectangular pond with footbridges and flowerbeds surrounded by 16th-century chequer-board *azulejo* tiles. The circular marble fountain in the centre of the pond was demolished in 1833 'twelve' Jeronimite monasteries – a symbolic and sacred number *par excellence* suggesting a pious devotion to Christology, the branch of theology concerned with the person, attributes and deeds of Christ. The goal was never realized but it is nevertheless true that the various existing monasteries and those founded subsequently ended up complying with the king's wishes. Hermitages were enlarged to give them a more traditional monastic dimension and to confer upon them the dignity that the king believed they deserved. The expansion of existing religious houses and the foundation of new ones continued during the reign of John III. By the mid-sixteenth century, Jeronimite communities were established at the Mosteiro de Penha Longa and the Mosteiro da Pena at Sintra, São Jerónimo do Mato at Alenquer, São Marcos at Tentúgal, Nossa Senhora do Espinheiro, near Évora, the Mosteiro de Berlengas (which later moved to Vale Benfeito, near Peniche), Santa Marinha da Costa (which previously belonged to the Observant Order) and the Restelo chapel. This, as we know, belonged to the Order of Christ but was handed over to the Jeronimites in exchange for the site of the synagogue in Lisbon, which later became Nossa Senhora da Conceição dos Freires. The chapel was to make way for the splendid Mosteiro de Santa Maria de Belém, more commonly known as the Mosteiro dos Jerónimos.

The spiritual life of the Jeronimites within the cloister was one of contemplation. Probably their most significant contribution to the creation of a more modern form of Christian devotion was to promote the life of Jesus as the example for human morality and to proclaim the joy to be found in emulating him. The decorative scheme on the ground floor of the cloister seems to be connected to this fundamental aspect of monastic life. Jeronimite monks attached great importance to the practice of 'internal' prayer and the power of the images encouraged mystical participation in Christ's life and Passion. This régime of contemplation and the study of Neoplatonic doctrine would bear fruit in the work and writings of Heitor Pinto, who took his vows at the Mosteiro dos Jerónimos in 1543. He was the author of what Sylvie Deswarte calls 'a genuine bestseller' in the field of contemporary religious literature: *A Imagem da Vida Cristã* (The Vision of Christian Life) written in 1563. Some scholars believe that the book provided the inspiration for the Platonic and Mannerist poetry of Luís de Camões.

WORK BEGINS AT SANTA MARIA DE BELÉM

THE WORK OF DIOGO BOITACA

A monument like the Mosteiro dos Jerónimos is not built in a day. Transport delays, planning problems, operational difficulties, changes of architect, accidents, political wrangling and, quite simply, lack of money and the massive scale of the project all meant that work fell behind schedule. At various times, the words 'permanent building site' were used in progress reports by several of the monastery's leading historians, including José de Siguenza (1600–05), Diogo de Jesus (1655), Jacinto de São Miguel in 1721 and Manuel Bautista de Castro in the first half of the eighteenth century.

One chronicler, Diogo de Jesus, stated that the work had only reached 'a quarter of the original plan: of four cloisters only one is finished; of four dormitories, there is only one and that incomplete'. According to Ribeiro Guimarães, writing in 1872, there seems to have been a drawing or 'archetype' in the monastery's registry, which was lost when religious orders were abolished in 1834. It was drawn up by a certain Master Putacha (or Putaka), sometimes referred to as João Potazza. This Putacha can have been none other than the master builder Diogo Boitaca (or Boytac), whose name was Italianized in order to lend him the unique prestige that the seventeenth and eighteenth centuries accorded only to Italian architects.

The two largest construction stages of the Mosteiro dos Jerónimos are believed to have taken place during the reign of Manuel I. The first, which began in 1501 or 1502, was under the direction of Diogo Boitaca, a master builder of unknown descent. Despite his mythical Italian origins, some historians say he was from Germany or Central Europe or, more likely, from southern France. He first became active in the reign of John II. His contribution to the building can be divided into two periods: before 1513 and from 1514 onwards.

The second phase began in 1517 under the supervision of the Basque master builder João de Castilho.

There is documentary evidence that the first significant payments towards the project were made in 1502 or 1503, and that the Florentine banker and merchant Bartolomeu Marchione, who was also the king's financial adviser, was authorized to hand over monthly sums of 300 *cruzados* to the then 'overseer' or clerk of works, Pêro Travaços, appointed in 1501. Documents from 1505 give more details of the construction work, now under the control of the great Boitaca. They show details of deliveries of cartloads of stone from the quarries at Rio Seco, Ribeira da Ajuda and Alcolena, which were stored in the 'barns' of the Palace of Restelo. The names of some of the workers recorded here would reappear on the payroll nine years later.

This sense of continuity indicates that work advanced at a steady pace, at least immediately after the laying of the foundation stone. It seems certain that all the necessary measurements were calculated and the foundations laid, otherwise there would have been no reason to store blocks of dressed stone. An accurate site plan would have been necessary in order to install at least some of the extensive drainage system, an operation that was reportedly under way. As Rafael Moreira

View of the cloister, east
façade

Detail of a Manueline arch in the cloister: man with cudgel

concludes, this explains why, in one of his 'discourses' dated 1504, Pedro de Meneses referred in such glowing terms to the building the king was creating, and mentioned the multitude of craftsmen and labourers employed on the site – with around 100 working alongside Boitaca in 1514. It is also likely that, when the king bought plots of land in 1513, he did so with an already existing plan in mind (although when this was drawn up remains a mystery), with the intention to relaunch construction on a grander scale. The accounts for 1514 show frantic activity, with the delivery of large quantities of dressed 'white Alcolena stone' and 'black Restello stone' destined for the church.

Quite apart from more ancient evidence, we can be fairly sure that construction work took on added momentum around 1513, perhaps due to a change in or enforcement of political will. From 1514 onwards, much more was achieved and the workforce increased. So too did the number of master builders and ornamental sculptors until finally, in 1517, the project underwent a major rethink. The king appointed a new architect and changed the specification, in order to extend the building and redesign it in a manner more suited to his personal taste, probably a new style that was gradually developing.

Among the parts of the project completed by 1516, a number were carried out under Diogo Boitaca's supervision. They include the large dormitory block laid from east to west and the arcade of the porch beneath it. Even after restoration, the vaulted ceilings reveal technical details typical of the master. The original chancel, believed to have had a straight end, was certainly high and vaulted. The walls of the main body of the church also rose to a great height. The windows and some parts of the roof supports, such as the twisted half-columns, were prepared; some were installed while others were ready for installation. The north and south chapels off the transept, with square, straight-ribbed vaulting, were presumably already built. So too was the basic structure of the columns along the nave, reaching up to the level where the ribs began. However, one of the church's most important features – the vaulted ceiling above the transept and the nave – was still to be constructed.

The cloister was partly built and some of the ground-floor ceiling completed. The external façades had cylindrical buttresses typical of Boitaca's design, which as Reinaldo dos Santos points out, were decorated at a later stage.

There appears to be no doubt that Diogo Boitaca was responsible for the overall plan of the building and its elevations. The Mosteiro dos Jerónimos is a larger version of the plan for the enlargement of the Convento de Jesus at Setúbal. Each of the two buildings was intended from the outset to be a great monastic house served by a large hall church. The main body of the church would have three vaulted naves with eight pillars (those in the transept having a larger circumference), an upper choir into which the final two pillars would be integrated, and a lower choir with four chapels and a central aisle, at right angles to the western entrance. The transept would be an innovation, not only for the vastness of its surface area and its spaciousness, but also because the plan provided for two chapels at the south and north ends, as well as the chancel. The chapels with their barrel vaults and the chancel with its groined vault would be of similar proportions so that the decorations could be exactly the same.

Like that of the Convento de Jesus at Setúbal built by Boitaca ten years earlier, the church's south wall was to have a monumental buttressed portal facing the seashore. As well as giving access to the church, it would provide additional support to the wall, which was thinner at this point and not sturdy enough to support the internal vaulting. However, Boitaca would not be the one to build it.

The north wall was considerably thicker, with exactly twelve confessionals and twelve cells at ground level. The twelve confessionals led off the church and lower choir, while the twelve cells were off the cloister. Twelve is a symbolic number *par excellence* and once again alludes to the life of Christ. Inside the wall an enclosed staircase (a common feature of military architecture) led to the upper choir and the roof. The whole project was a much larger and more complex version of the Convento de Jesus.

In 1516, when '*m.te boytaqua*' was still in charge, dressed stone blocks were delivered to the site from the quarries at Raposeira and Vinhas. At this time, different craftsmen were working on specific decorative motifs. The records list them piece by piece, in the singular, for example, 'artichoke', 'gargoyle', '*chambrante*', 'twist', 'capital', 'twisted *chambrante*', 'large column', 'knot' for 'upper moulding' or 'lower moulding', and 'Roman'. It is not always clear what these terms mean. There were, of course, many carved gargoyles, and 'twist' referred to the spiral stone columns of which Boitaca was so fond, or possibly to a part of a continuous section of a cornice or frieze. '*Chambrante*' (sometimes written *chambrente*) was probably derived from the French *chambrette* (a type of pear) and presumably meant a corbel or bracket, which in some instances would be in the form of a spiral, and obviously referred to the semi-conical, 'pear' shape of these elements. 'Artichoke', meanwhile, is related to the tradition known in Portugal as '*alcachofrado*', an embossing technique used in embroidery and tapestry to create plant designs. In this context, it probably meant plant motifs carved from pieces of stone for use on door jambs and ornamental friezes. 'Capital' referred to the top of a column. 'Roman' is an enigmatic term which may have meant any motif in the Classical or Antique style but usually would have meant part or all of a frieze with plant motifs, since the term was used in this precise sense as late as the eighteenth century.

'Knot' would not have had anything to do with the favourite Manueline knotted rope motif, of which there are practically none at Belém, but to the floral rosettes used to decorate window arches.

THE WORK OF JOÃO DE CASTILHO

Boitaca never managed to carry out the work. In April 1516, João de Castilho came on the scene and worked alongside Boitaca before taking full control of the site on 2 January 1517. After this, Diogo Boitaca's name does not reappear on any document. There are probably two reasons for this. Firstly, he was in disgrace with the king following the military disaster at Mármora for which the monarch held Boitaca responsible. This was because Boitaca was a famously pig-headed individual who probably insisted on doing things the old-fashioned way, despite technical advances in military architecture. Secondly, there were major problems with the roof. Castilho had already worked for the Portuguese crown and roofs and ceilings were his speciality, as can be seen from his earlier projects such as Braga Cathedral (1509), Viseu Cathedral (1513) and the Convento de Cristo at Tomar (1515). His move to southern Portugal played an important role in the gradual adoption during the reign of Manuel I of the Spanish Plateresque style – so called because of its resemblance to the art of the silversmith or *platero* – favoured by master builders from the Basque provinces of northern Spain, where Castelho was born.

Around this time, the king created a new set of rules governing how the project for the Mosteiro dos Jerónimos should proceed. A Papal Bull issued on 17 July 1517, named the monastery as the mother house of the Jeronimite Order in Portugal, designed to accommodate 100 monks. Clearly, things were about to change. Meanwhile, under the terms of King Manuel's will, drawn up in April that year, the monastery was to become the royal mausoleum, finally overriding any claim to that role by the rotunda built by King Duarte at Batalha. Significantly, the will was written only a month after the death of the king's second wife, Maria, which must have influenced the monarch's decision to make the building an even more splendid memorial to the late queen (hence the statues sculpted by Chanterêne for the west door, which are actual portraits).

In 1517, with Castilho now in charge of the site, efforts were redoubled. He co-ordinated work on the 'first cloister and chapel and sacristy and side door', and divided the tasks among a workforce of 110. Castilho and thirty French, Flemish, Spanish and Portuguese workers started on the south portal. This was a priority, since the portal would act as brace for the roof. A Spaniard Pero Guterres and a team of twenty-seven men – all of them Spanish – prepared the chapter house. Rodrigo de Pontezilha and four fellow Spaniards concentrated purely on the chapter house door. Another Spaniard Fernando de la Fremosa led a group of twenty working on the sacristy, while his compatriot Francisco de Benavente and his team of thirty-eight were assigned to the cloister and probably also worked on the church. The French sculptor Nicolau Chanterêne, whose status as a prestigious artist meant he was particularly well paid, and eleven mostly French craftsmen, were together responsible for the west door. Pêro de Trillo, also Spanish, and thirty-eight artisans worked on the cloister staircase, while the Portuguese Felipe Henriques – son of Mateus Fernandes – and fifty-five workers also were assigned to the cloister. Another Portuguese Leonardo Vaz and fifteen craftsmen worked on the refectory, with João Gonçalves and ten craftsmen tackling three choir chapels, a task they shared with Rodrigo Afonso and his team of ten artisans.

This ability to make optimum use of human resources and to organize the work on site so effectively shows that João de Castilho was more than just a master builder. He was a genuine contractor in the modern sense of the word, a construction engineer, personnel manager and project co-ordinator. The key to his success was his skill in dealing with large numbers of workers – sometimes there were as many as 250 people engaged simultaneously on the project – and in

View inside the refectory (Filipe Henriques, c.1517)

choosing and managing sub-contractors, like Filipe Henriques and Leonardo Vaz who had previously worked for Boitaca at Belém and were now given bigger and better assignments.

The 'companies' put together by João de Castilho were very productive, both on the construction of the various sections of the building and in devising its architectural vocabulary. They added the roof to the ground floor of the cloister and began the construction of the upper floor of what was to be Portugal's first vaulted, two-storey cloister. They finished the job in record time, partly because of the contributions of a group of trusted craftsmen who had worked with Castilho on projects further north. They included Juan de la Faya, André Pilarte, Machim and Diogo de Castilho – João's youngest brother. This proves how mobile the artisans were, and further evidence is provided by documents relating to the Norman sculptor Nicolau Chanterêne's work on the west door. It seems likely that the two of the many colleagues named 'Martim', 'Guilherme' or 'Guilhelme' were Martim Blas and Guillén Colas, master stonecarvers who would be involved in the building of the Cathedral of Santiago de Compostela in the 1520s. Nicolau also created sculptures for the Royal Hospital in the same Spanish city. João de Castilho was responsible for the decoration of the large pillars in the church. Under his leadership, his colleagues would build the sacristy with a

(Opposite) South wing of the cloister, doors leading to the cells or confessionals

Double window lighting the enclosed staircase, which leads to the upper choir

single central pillar and rib-vaulting in the shape of palm leaves, the portal and part of the walls of the chapter house (left unfinished), and the refectory – a large, unified, well-lit space with some fine architectural features. Its vaulted ceiling was executed by Leonardo Vaz in the style of Boitaca, with that architect's characteristic central net effect, created by juxtaposing ribs to form a series of trapeziums. João de Castilho also carried out the complex task of constructing the ceilings above the nave and the transept, whose design reveals both English and Spanish influences. The ceilings show considerable technical audacity. Not only do they cover an immense space, they are also highly innovative in that Castilho used unusually slender ribs arranged in such a way as to produce a 'spiderweb' effect, rather than the usual florid stars. This enabled him to create a unified space in the church with a triple nave leading to the transept. This huge hall-church was the first of its kind in Portugal.

The brilliance of the work, completed in 1522, shows Castilho to have been a genuine master of the art of roof and ceiling construction. From the time he began practising his craft in northern Portugal, he always took with him a team of co-workers whose task it was to adorn basic structures with sculptures and other decorations, presumably dictated by the iconographic scheme demanded by their clients. This is probably one of the reasons why he was chosen for the Jerónimos. His reputation as a master builder with a talent for finding solutions to difficult roofing problems, and as an astute project manager, would have preceded him. As construction progressed, his work took an interesting, new, stylistic turn and, by the 1530s, he had taken on board the then current trend for reviving the forms of Classical Antiquity. Entirely self-taught, he became a fully-fledged Renaissance architect. This notable achievement typified João de Castilho's way of doing things. He gradually developed from master mason to architect in the modern sense of the word. He became rich enough to marry and his skill became something of a legend.

At the Mosteiro dos Jerónimos, his personal trademark is clear to see. As well as finding solutions to structural problems, João de Castilho created a new vocabulary for monumental architecture, so changing, even transfiguring, its outward appearance. The work at the monastery

(Opposite) Church interior showing the building to be of uniform height on the linesof a *Hallenkirch* or hall-church

View of contrasting forms on the upper storey, showing the cylindrical structure of Diogo de Boitaca's original pilasters, later added to by João de Castilho and Torralva

carried out under Boitaca was probably closer to the more typical image of Manueline architecture of central Portugal. The Manueline style that took hold in the first decade of the sixteenth century was characterized by open spaces, cylindrical structural supports, keel arches and Moorish or Mudejar ornamentation, especially in the larger spaces. The decorations were hyper-naturalistic, fleshy and elaborately carved. Apart from Boitaca, other master builders contributed to the development of the style, including Mateus Fernandes, responsible for Nossa Senhora do Pópulo at Caldas da Rainha (1505) and the portico of the so-called *Capelas Imperfeitas* (Unfinished Chapels) at the monastery of Batalha (1509), and Diogo de Arruda, who built the choir at the Convento de Cristo, Tomar, (1510–13).

Castilho and master builders of the Basque Provinces led a change in taste. Their constructions were influenced by the Flamboyant style of the late Gothic period, seen throughout Europe. Their ornamentation, however, bore little resemblance to the rather crude naturalism of the early Manueline period. They preferred instead the Spanish Plateresque, which in turn drew on the Classical architecture of Ancient Rome.

Spanish Plateresque ornamentation had much in common with the Lombard style of northern Italy, with its grotesque figures, mouldings and fillets. Its echoes of the Classical era, such as door jambs adorned with medallions and busts, also paved the way for the introduction of Renaissance-style decoration. In late Gothic and earlier Manueline buildings, ornamentation of this kind would be mounted on blank walls, or in other empty spaces. But Castelho and his contemporaries created even greater harmony by using spiral ribs and the bulbous, naturalistic motifs for which Manueline reliefs are famous. A classic example of this felicitous and versatile combination is the portal at Tomar, which Castilho completed immediately before taking up his post at Belém. The door has three archivolts: the two outer ones decorated with characteristically simple 'Manueline'

(Top) Cloisters: detail of central pillars of window arch

(Right) Cloister: detail of central pillar of window arch

motifs, while the interior one, whose commemorative plaque bears Castilho's signature, has a vertical, Renaissance-style sequence of goblets, medallions and trophies. The same decorative scheme is systematically repeated at the Jerónimos – for example, on the chapter-house door, the central pillar of the sacristy, on the pillars of the church itself and especially on the outer walls of the cloister.

With the Mosteiro dos Jerónimos as its epicentre, the powerful wave of Spanish influence sweeping over Portuguese architecture was, as Rafael Moreira contends, well suited to King Manuel's political ambitions. Architecture provided an effective and concrete statement of his desire to unite the crowns of the Iberian Peninsula. It was no accident that, in the reign of Manuel I, the iconographic language of the buildings commissioned by the monarch, became so truly magnificent both in terms of its symbolic meaning and in the quality of execution, and was popularly described as being *ad modum yspaniae* (in the Spanish style).

IN THE CLASSICAL STYLE

Political change and ideological shifts had an impact on the monastery's architecture. The succession to the throne of King John III had serious consequences. John, it seems, was not interested in continuing his father's legacy and was even downright hostile to the idea. Instead, the new king preferred to commission further major improvements to the Convento de Cristo at Tomar, where he initiated a series of grandiose projects. Here a different architectural and decorative language, rooted in Renaissance Classicism, was brought into play. Work in the Manueline style, completed only a short time before, was hidden behind new additions in the new taste. The monarch also expressed his desire to be buried in the chapel of Nossa Senhora da Conceição, a little Renaissance jewel, among the finest on the Iberian Peninsula. He abandoned the idea of making the Mosteiro dos Jerónimos the mausoleum of the Avis-Beja dynasty, a decision that went against the will of his father. Unsurprisingly, around 1530, João de Castilho, the greatest contemporary royal architect, was transferred from the site at Belém (where work had ground to a halt) to design and direct the new and important Tomar project.

John III's cultural and religious philosophy was completely opposed to that of his predecessor. He was highly sympathetic to the concept of *devotio moderna*, (new devotion), and other progressive ways of thinking. Architecture responded to these new ideas by adopting a Classical vocabulary 'in the Roman manner' – a radical move away from the late Gothic models that inspired the Manueline style. On the other side of the coin were the religious reforms initiated by the king and largely carried out by Jeronimite monks. For ten years, until the stronger winds of the Catholic Counter-Reformation began to blow, the Jeronimites exerted a very powerful influence on royal construction policy. As Renaissance became the officially accepted architectural style, there appears to have been no alternative but to reflect the prevailing taste in all the phases of building at the monastery.

At this point, the architect Diogo de Torralva was appointed 'master of the works at Belém', a post he held from 1540 until 1551. His basic task was to co-ordinate the completion of the various half-built sections of the monastery, and to add the finishing touches. His contribution can best be seen in the previously unfinished north and west sides of upper storey of the cloister. Here, the keystones are plainer, with 'Roman' ornamentation, but most striking of all are the architraves, decorated with busts of imperial-looking figures and diamond-shaped plaques filled with reliefs of triumphs (festive processions celebrating the victories of Roman generals), which are among Portugal's most interesting examples of Renaissance Classicism. These simple designs encapsulate the alternative vision that Torralva brought to the structure of the monastery, without disturbing the harmony of the surrounding architecture. Torralva was also given the job of constructing a

Architrave with Renaissance decoration, executed while Diogo de Torralva was 'master of the works' (c.1540–51)

Architrave in the cloister: Renaissance decoration with suits of armour, 'triumphs', *tondi* and mythological figures

Architrave in the cloister
with Renaissance decora-
tions, which contrast with
the Manueline arches on
the upper storey.

(Opposite)
Grasshopper gargoyle

Renaissance architrave, showing the interplay between the flat surface adorned with *tondi*, and plaques with Classical images, as well as Boitaca's circular buttress with its Renaissance ornamentation

Architrave in the cloister with Renaissance decorations

Detail of a choir stall

(Opposite) Detail of
first-row choir stall

new main door, although this was replaced in the seventeenth century. He also drew up the plan for the choir stalls in the upper choir, a beautiful example of the woodcarver's art, exquisitely executed by Diego de Sarça. Torralva was also responsible for adapting the chancel to accommodate the remains of Manuel I, which were initially laid to rest in Henry the Navigator's original chapel; this was still intact, presumably in the grounds of the monastery, to the left of the present main door.

More Renaissance touches were added to the monastery by Torralva's successor, Jerónimo de Ruão (1531–1601), who also completed the project. Jerónimo de Ruão was the son of the sculptor João de Ruão, famed for the large body of work he produced, mostly in the Coimbra region, and for being one of the first to introduce Renaissance aesthetics to Portugal. Jerónimo was appointed 'master of the works of the monastery' in 1563, and worked until his death designing and oversee-ing several different phases of construction. He is buried in the cloister. His most important assignment was the reconstruction of the chancel, commissioned in 1563 by King John's consort Queen Catharine. The queen wished to replace the Manueline chancel because it was 'small and low', in other words similar to the chapels leading off the transept. Work began in around 1565 and was completed in 1572. The Mannerist style of the chancel marks a breakaway from the rest of the monastery and creates a complete contrast. Bombastic Manueline monumentalism made way for plain, austere, rigorous and rectilinear Classicism. The theory of Classical orders is applied to create a feeling of rhythm and harmony, with Corinthian pillars on the upper level and Ionic pillars at ground level. The interplay of black, white and red marble lends an atmosphere of nobility and solemnity to a space intended as a family mausoleum. The barrel-vaulted ceiling terminates in a semicircular apse, supported by the concave end wall. The ornamented ribs of the vaulting extend

Detail of a misericord in
the choir stalls

to form a frame for the panels of the altarpiece. A corridor in the side walls leads to two spiral staircases giving access to the wall behind the altarpiece. Viewed from the outside, the chancel appears
solid and impenetrable, like a piece of military architecture, with its lancet windows and staircases
resembling watch-towers. The 'military' image of the chancel, shared with so much Portuguese
architecture of the last quarter of the sixteenth century, bore clear connotations of the Counter-
Reformation. Like any sacred building, it also represented the 'fortress of the soul'.

Choir stalls

THE 'MANUELINE' STYLE AND REVIVALISM

THE INVENTION OF THE 'MANUELINE STYLE'

The unique hybrid that came to be known as Manueline architecture, was largely the result of João de Castilho's collaboration with Boitaca and other Portuguese master builders on projects in the southern Spanish region of Estremadura and the south of Portugal. It was a style that would reach its zenith at the Mosteiro dos Jerónimos.

Strangely, the term 'Manueline style' was not coined until 300 years later by Francisco Adolfo Varnhagen in his short but influential study of the Jeronimite monastery, entitled *Notícia Histórica e Descriptiva do Mosteiro de Belém* (Historical and Descriptive Notes on the Monastery of Belém), published in 1842. In his little book, Varnhagen compares the monastery to other buildings dating from the reign of Manuel I and finds many features in common. He then proceeds to classify them under the heading 'Manueline' (or 'Emmanueline') architecture.

Varnhagen lists 'ten defining characteristics' of the Manueline style: the predominance of the semicircular and depressed arch over pointed arches; tolerance of other types of arch; polystile (or multiple) pillars; the extravagant forms of such pillars; the absence of straight mouldings; vertical surfaces interspersed with niches, statues and canopies; doorways with composite door-posts, sometimes with repeating shapes set at an angle; the 'abhorrence' of simple repetition and lack of symmetry; the use of octagonal shapes; the use of ornate, flower-like motifs and royal emblems.

In listing these defining characteristics, with considerable insight Varnhagen concentrated only on the most visible aspects of decoration – rather than structure. However, he did recognize the formal unity and 'family likeness' of buildings commissioned by King Manuel. It was also an auspicious moment – the beginning of the Romantic period – to produce an historical and aesthetic study of this nature and to create an ideological debate. It was the fashion at this time to regard architectural styles as symbols of national identity, as tangible and durable expressions of the spirit of a people. Varnhagen (born in Brazil of a Portuguese mother and German father) was steeped in the romantic, progressive, liberal nationalism typical of the mid-nineteenth century. As such, he credited the Portuguese people with their own national style, which reached its heyday during the reign of Manuel I, so coinciding with the glory days of maritime exploration and discovery, and imperial expansion.

The term 'Manueline architecture' quickly became common currency among the Portuguese intelligentsia. It was adopted both by eminent archaeologists like Luís Mouzinho de Albuquerque, then engaged on major restorations at Batalha, and writers such as João Batista de Almeida Garrett and Alexandre Herculano whose work spread it to a wider audience. Manueline architecture enjoyed and continues to enjoy national and international prominence.

The concept also appealed to more radical Romantic nationalists such as the French historian Edgar Quinet. Writing from memory in 1857, Quinet enthusiastically described what he saw – or thought he saw – in Portugal.

(Left) Medallion in the moulding of a corner of the cloister: a black man, c.1515

(Right) Manueline arch in the cloister: detail of the fantasy figure of a dragon, c.1515

(Far right) Manueline arch in the cloister: two lizards or salamanders with knotted tails, c.1515

This is God's house, but it is adorned like a ship about to set sail. On entering the church, one sees the fruits and plants of newly discovered continents, harvested and gathered together in *bas-reliefs* . . . Here, Gothic sirens swim in an alabaster sea; there, climbing apes from the Ganges swing at the end of the nave of the church of São Pedro. Ostriches from Brazil flap their wings around the Cross of Golgotha. Tears flow from coats of arms. Marble *mappae mundi*, astrolabes and set-squares appear alongside crucifixes, nautical axes, shields and ladders. . .

This exaggerated, distorted idea of the architecture of the Manueline period, clearly fed by its associations with the great voyages of discovery, became widespread in the nineteenth century among travellers and the educated classes. For better or worse, the Manueline style could not escape its nautical and exotic connotations, which were exploited in 1842 by Prince Ferdinand of Saxe-Coburg, consort of Queen Maria II, when he commissioned his eccentric, revivalist Castelo da Pena at Sintra. Critics, aesthetes and historians in Portugal and elsewhere shared this peculiar view and turned their attention to trying to unravel the Manueline style's potent but impenetrable iconography. Because of Portuguese contact with the Orient, it was easy enough to create the myth that 'the ravishing splendour of Indian architecture' was reflected 'in many important buildings' with 'details reproduced not only from India but also from the Far East', as Albrecht Haupt wrote in 1891. With the publication in 1952 of Reinaldo dos Santos's splendid book *O Estilo Manuelino* (The Manueline Style), the connection between Manueline architecture and the era of maritime adventure was formally acknowledged. The author described the characteristic features of the architec-

ture as having 'an exuberant naturalism' and recognized 'the predominance of certain themes evoking the sea and the insignia of the crown'. He dubs Manueline 'the style of the voyages of discovery'.

Not all historians agreed, however. Some of different philosophical persuasions, including the late nineteenth-century Positivists, contested this nationalistic interpretation of the Manueline style. Some, quite reasonably, disputed its nautical symbolism. In fact, most of the elements taken to be references to seafaring were no such thing. They were simply variations of a type of ornamentation commonly seen in other buildings of the period, both in neighbouring Spain, where the famous Isabeline Gothic style flourished, and in the rest of Europe. The Manueline style was an offshoot of the late Gothic from which it derived all its structural elements and many of its decorative schemes. Certainly, some aspects were accentuated to reflect the political and economic climate in Portugal during the age of discovery. As we shall discover, it is now clear that all the maritime symbols such as ropes, fish, anchors and ships in the Mosteiro dos Jerónimos are in the parts of the building that have been restored at various times. The nineteenth-century restorers accepted the notion that Manueline architecture represented Portugal's seafaring history, hence the exaggerations and anachronisms that helped perpetuate the erroneous myth.

Nevertheless, it is precisely because Manueline architecture and decoration has become so deeply rooted in the nation's consciousness that it has endured for so many years. It is also because the Manueline, particularly in its most revolutionary and eloquent manifestations, is so different from other architectural style. How did this come about? In the period between 1490 and

Manueline arch in the
cloister: centaur

around 1530, Portugal was a melting pot of different architectural influences. All over the land, a whole series of principles, styles, endlessly diverse ideas about decoration and indecision about the interpretation of figurative motifs, would all come together in a single region, or even in a single building. Manueline architecture resulted from the availability of choice. Some architects opted to continue the traditions of the fifteenth century and international Gothic, either by creating original designs or copying existing ones. Others chose to follow the Flamboyant style – known in Portugal as 'the English style'. Some architectural projects incorporated Mudejar or Moorish motifs, while others combined ideas from the Mediterranean and northern Europe, or adopted other ornamental styles of the Renaissance, like Spanish Plateresque. To all of this was added the incredible weight of heraldic Manueline iconography.

The term invented in the nineteenth century allowed restorers complete freedom to appropriate and reinterpret Manueline architecture. The restorers of the Mosteiro dos Jerónimos took full advantage of that freedom.

REVIVALISM

As civil war raged in Portugal, troops occupied the Mosteiro dos Jerónimos. After religious orders were abolished by the decree of 28 December 1833, the monastery lay abandoned until it was handed over to the Casa Pia, a large charitable institution.

Twenty-six years later, witnessing the dilapidated state of the great building and the primitive conditions under which the charity was obliged to operate, the superintendent of Casa Pia, Eugénio de Almeida, proposed that the monastery be adapted to suit the needs of charity workers and those in their care. Having studied the superintendent's report, delivered in 1859, the Ministry of Public Works decided to launch a major building programme, to enable the charity to work in a dignified manner. The project also won the support of Prince Ferdinand.

Plateresque grotesque on a pilaster in the cloister

(Following page) View of the former 'dormitory block' after restoration in the 19th and early 20th century (in the centre, the entrance to the National Museum of Archaeology)

In January 1860, the French architect Jean Colson was contracted to produce a plan for the conversion and restoration of the monastery. For two years, Colson worked intensively, producing seventeen drawings and a range of options for 'finishing' the building, all based on a revivalist aesthetic. They proposed various ways of extending, rearranging and decorating the monastery, and some of the proposals were adopted in later plans. Colson, however, was dismissed shortly afterwards.

From then on, the history of the project was stormy, uncertain and even tragic. After Colson's departure, Valentim José Correia took over between 1863 and 1865, when he was replaced by an Englishman Samuel Bennett (1865–67), who had worked on the second and final version of the Palacete de Monserrate at Sintra. Bennett did not succeed in bringing any of his somewhat incongruous plans to fruition, although the seeds of some of his ideas were later recycled by his successors. His replacements were Aquiles Rambois and Giuseppe Cinatti, set designers at Lisbon's Teatro de São Carlos.

Between 1867 and 1878, Rambois and Cinatti changed the dynamic of the restoration, a process carried even further by the various architects who succeeded them. They worked at high speed, with no expense spared, as they set about remodelling and restoring the dormitory block, introducing strong vertical lines which lent it a symmetry never intended in the original. Following similar principles, they added a finishing touch to the building with a 'formal' façade at the western end. The most absurd addition of all was an Indian-style dome shaped like a bishop's mitre, raised above the choir of church. It replaced the typically late-Gothic, pyramidal bell-tower, deemed too modest to celebrate the mighty Vasco da Gama and his exploits. Halfway along the side of the building running parallel to the river, the two scenery designers proposed to erect the three-sided tower with four pinnacles, an idea that owed more to the Gothic than to the neo-Manueline revival. Predictably, this part of the project was severely criticized for its eccentric proportions. When the partially built tower collapsed in 1878, killing about ten workers, there was a nationwide scandal and the two Italians were promptly fired. As Ramalho Ortigão so crushingly put it, the tower 'unable to collapse from old age, collapsed from shame'. His words simply served to highlight the

Detail of tracery around one of the cloister arches: a ship, probably carved in the 18th century during restoration

(Right) Aerial view of the Praça do Império

controversy that surrounded the venture from the outset, with Possidónio Silva drawing up alternative plans in 1867, illustrated by a magnificent wooden scale model and with the Brazilian Varnhagen commenting on the various options.

The 'restored' Mosteiro dos Jerónimos looks like a piece of scenery devised by set designers, adhering to very nineteenth-century practices and ideology. They made the dormitory wing a monotonously regular structure, intended to provide a multi-purpose space. Also lost forever were the Renaissance porch and the even more beautiful Sala dos Reis, or Room of the Kings, a work in the Classical style, whose austerity was regarded as phoney, anti-medieval, anti-Manueline and, worst of all, anti-Romantic. It was demolished to create the present empty space between the body of the church and the dormitory, ridding the church of what contemporaries apparently considered an eyesore.

Rafael Cardoso and Raimundo Valadas succeeded the Italians, but work came to a standstill again in 1894. Adães Bermudes and Marques da Silva also tried to intervene. A national competition was launched but to no avail. Finally a plan by Parente da Silva, drawn up in the first decade of the twentieth century, put an end to the controversy, and work on the ruined main block was finally completed. Delayed decisions, disagreements between various architects, the damage and disturbance caused by the permanent building site that the monastery had become, also contributed to the debate surrounding 'Manueline style'. The efforts of the two scene painters remain a living testimony to a dubious interpretation of the style. The shell, anchor and sailing ship motifs adorning the doorposts and fanlights in the dormitories, pass – or at least used to pass – for 'originals', so forcing the 'Manueline' (or as the poet and essayist Abílio Guerra Junqueiro ironically dubbed it, 'sub-Manueline') to be forever linked to the famous maritime symbolism.

The durability of Manueline architecture and decoration would be proven by the number of twentieth-century revivalist projects inspired by the style. Late Romantic revivalism became associated with the commemoration of events of national importance, such as the wave of patriotism

that followed the British Ultimatum of 1890 – threatening war if the Portuguese did not withdraw from Rhodesia – and its influence continued during the early part of the twentieth century. The style was stamped on public festivities and trade fairs, and manifested itself in various forms in Portuguese pavilions and even on allegorical floats, like Simões de Almeida's *Art* and Rafael Bordalo Pinheiro's *War*, which paraded through the street during the commemoration of the 300th anniversary of the death of Portugal's great poet Luís de Camões in 1880.

It was no accident that the Mosteiro dos Jerónimos became a great patriotic monument. The nautical symbolism, allegedly germane to Manueline style, became automatically associated with the celebration of Portugal's poets and thinkers. The monastery stood as a memorial to the great discoverers and to some degree reverted to the purpose for which it was built. This is why the tombs of the poet Luís de Camões and Vasco da Gama stand side by side under the choir of the church, and Alexandre Herculano, Portuguese Romantic poet and champion of social change, is buried in the chapter house. The impressive World Exhibition of 1940 was staged right in front of the monastery. Salazar chose the monument as the splendid backdrop to celebrations of his dictatorship. Finally in 1985 the remains of the poet Fernando Pessoa were transferred to the cloister, as if in response to the words of his mythical cycle of poems *Mensagem* (Message), a cathartic synthesis of the religious history of Portugal.

THE SOUTH PORTAL

The monastery's southern façade is set parallel to the river, facing the seashore. From left to right, four main sections are apparent.

The first consists of the former dormitory and the arcades beneath, which have undergone a series of restorations. The building is now home to the National Museum of Archaeology and part of the collection of the Maritime Museum.

Then comes the church itself with its massive naves. Windows are set along the length of the façade whose most striking feature is the magnificent south portal.

The exterior of the transept looks like a box with chamfered edges, a device to reinforce the angles of the walls and support the massive weight of the ceiling. The simple rectangular structure on the end, with an *œil de bœuf* window, is the south arm of the transept.

Next is the Mannerist chancel, which, unlike the other sections, with their Manueline friezes and moulded cornices, has no external decoration. The main body of the church is topped with ironwork rosettes.

As noted above, the turrets topped with a cupola date from the nineteenth century. The original was a simple octagonal Manueline bell-tower with an eight-sided roof.

The elegant tracery of the portal, the rhythmic nature of the mouldings and the clear, bright colour of the white limestone all serve to counteract the awesome, monolithic impression of the south façade.

In terms of composition, the Mosteiro dos Jerónimos is one of Portugal's finest examples of late Gothic architecture. João de Castilho was responsible for the final design of what he called the 'side door'. Construction began in 1516 and took more than a year to complete. However, it seems certain that in his original drawings Diogo Boitaca provided for a side door to the monastery – a major innovation in a religious establishment for men.

Providing a solid canvas for the sumptuous ornamentation, the portal extends upwards over two storeys and is framed by two buttresses. At ground level is the double entrance door, topped by two tympanums with a large fanlight immediately above.

Since the walls are thinner on the south side of the church, the portal serves the additional purpose of shoring them up to support the weight of the vaulted ceiling. The original design for the portal was probably simpler, inspired by the example of the side door of the Convento de Jesus at Setúbal, also attributed to Boitaca. However, when it reached the construction stage, Castilho revised his drawings to include the ornamentation, which was typical of his works in that it combined late-Gothic aesthetics and his own version of the Spanish Plateresque. He had to allow for a far more complex, more narrative and doctrinaire iconography than originally envisaged. The monastery standing triumphantly facing the sea at Restelo was to be a glorious tribute to Portuguese exploits. The resemblance between the portal and the beautiful gold Monstrance of Belém (preserved in the National Museum of Medieval Art), cannot be ignored. Despite the differences of scale, the two more or less contemporary works of art are each a perfect expression of the

(Opposite) South portal (João de Castilho, 1517)

The Mosteiro dos Jerónimos seen from the east, with the Mannerist chancel in the foreground

aesthetics of the Manueline period. The most likely explanation of the similarities between them is that master masons and master goldsmiths were in the habit of passing their drawings around among themselves.

THE SYMBOLISM OF THE SOUTH PORTAL

The decorations on the south portal at Belém share the same imagery as the south portal at Tomar, completed by João de Castilho in 1515. Ecclesiastical art and architecture of the period drew on a textbook series of images reflecting contemporary religious concerns.

The saints depicted vary from place to place, but by analysing the attributes of each holy figure, a standard cast of characters is easy to identify.

In the centre of the portal is an image of Our Lady of Bethlehem and the Infant Jesus, holding a vessel containing the gifts of the Magi. Lower down, on the doorposts, is a hierarchical arrangement of the Twelve Apostles, some of them clearly recognizable by their particular attributes. St Peter and St Paul appear on the lower part of the buttress, symbolizing their role as 'pillars of the Church'. John the Baptist and the Apostles, James the Less, Thomas, Simon and Bartholomew are the easiest to spot. On the trumeau or central pier, is a statue of Henry the Navigator in armour, restored after one of the earthquakes devastated Lisbon in the sixteenth century. The original statue probably held a sword aloft like the images on tombs. As Damião de Góis tells us, at the 'side door facing the shore' King Manuel 'ordered that a statue of Prince Henry, who inspired these voyages, be carved in solid stone and placed on the central pier of the door, wearing a coat of mail, unsheathed sword raised high, in the manner of all the Kings and Princes whose feats of arms led them to victory'. Here the statue commemorates the monarch's ancestor who also founded the chapel of Restelo. Moreover, Manuel was Prince Henry's adopted grandson and, in many respects, his heir. He, like his grandfather, administered the Order of Christ. This memorial to the prince lends him heroic stature. Symbolically, this secular – as opposed to religious – figure stands right

(Right) Group of Apostles on the east side of the south portal

(Opposite) Statue of Henry the Navigator on the trumeau of the south portal

in the centre of the main door, serving as a unique 'keeper of the gates'. The two lions on the trumeau emphasize his function.

The tympanums show a series of scenes from the life of St Jerome. The saint is depicted wearing the vestments of a cardinal removing the thorn from the lion's paw, and as a hermit in the desert. Above, sheltered by canopies, are images of female saints, believed by many to represent the Four Sybils: St Catherine, St Apollonia, St Anastasia and St Lucy. On either side are the Prophets, Daniel, Ezekiel, Jeremiah and Isaiah. Above them are the Doctors and Fathers of the Church, with St Jerome and St Augustine on the left, and St Gregory the Great and St Ambrose on the right. The fanlight is surrounded by angels playing musical instruments, forming a truly Celestial Court. The small figure at the apex of the entrance arch is St Sebastian. At the very top, under an eighteenth-century baldachino, stands the Archangel Michael.

Thus, at the lowest level on the buttresses, we have the Twelve Apostles. Immediately above are the Four Prophets who foretold the coming of Christ. Above them are four crowned female figures. According to the interpretation of some historians, they represent four martyred saints, while others contend that they are the Four Sybils who prophesied the birth of the Messiah. Standing above them are the Virgin and Child, and the ecclesiastical figures of the four Doctors to complete the arrangement; they determined or interpreted biblical text and helped establish the Church as an institution. Presiding over the whole ensemble and dictating its overall meaning is Our Lady of Bethlehem.

Of the array of figures from the scriptures depicted on the portal, some, like the Prophets and possibly the Sybils, come from the Old Testament, while the Apostles and the Virgin Mary are from the New. Meanwhile, the Virgin and Child, prefigured in the Old Testament and appearing in the New, are sanctified in both scriptures. Standing at the very top of the portal, the image of the Archangel Michael, chosen by King Manuel in 1504 as 'guardian angel of the realm', acts as mediator, creating a miraculous connection between the temporal world of Henry the Navigator and the celestial realm. The portrayal of the Virgin and Child as links between the Old and New Testaments is a theological reference that becomes all the more meaningful in the context of a building occupied by the Jeronimite Order, a congregation at the forefront of pre-Reformation religious thought.

(Right) Lions at the base of the central trumeau of the south portal, which, with the figure of the Prince, represent the 'keepers of the gate'

(Opposite) south portal: double tympanum with bas-reliefs showing scenes from the life of St Jerome

We should also remember the Jeronimites' special devotion to the Virgin Mary, both as the protector of sailors and in her manifestation of Our Lady of Bethlehem. The monastery was founded on the feast of Epiphany, with the laying of the foundation stone on 6 January 1501 or 1502. The significant choice of date symbolized the far-sighted imperialism of King Manuel, who sought to make the monastery a 'New Bethlehem'. Largely through its association with the Christian mythology of the Three Kings, the monument came to represent the ideas of Portuguese expansionism and the conversion of the heathen.

Mary's role as the seafarer's guardian is particularly important in this context. As João Claro so eloquently stated in his book *Horas de nossa señora segundo costume romão com as horas do spirito sancto* (The Hours of the Virgin according to the Roman Custom and the Hours of the Holy Spirit), published in Paris in 1500, the Virgin was the 'true star of the sea'. The same epithet appears in other writings of the period such as Luís Anriquez's poem *Ave Mari'stela*, in Garcia de Resende's famous anthology of medieval Portuguese court poetry *Cancioneiro Geral*. More significantly still, in the funeral laments for the monarch, the name is repeated together with direct allusions to Bethlehem, emphasizing the role of the Virgin in the place the monarch had chosen to be entombed. Called 'Our Lady of the Three Kings' by the Master of the Order of Santiago, she was similarly invoked by the Count of Portalegre: 'Oh, Virgin who gave birth to God / near Jerusalem, / in the holy place of Bethlehem; . . . Oh Imperial Queen, / have mercy on him / to whom you owe more than to any other in Portugal'.

As well as providing a role model for mothers and women in general, the Virgin had a particularly devout following in a place where sailors came ashore from ships anchored in Lisbon harbour, and where she was acknowledged as the patron saint. It was fitting, therefore, that her blessing should be sought on the king's final resting place.

The hierarchical arrangement of the images adorning the portal suggests a more profound narrative content, which people at the time would have found easy to interpret because of its similarity to the liturgical dramas often performed by candlelight inside churches.

Also worth noticing, carved into the trumeau immediately below the plinth supporting Prince Henry, are six trade guild insignias, or 'citizen's coats of arms' – not to be confused with the traditional stonemason's marks. Some are incomplete but three are dated 1554, 1564 and 1639

(Previous pages) Sculpted figures of female saints and martyrs on the buttress of the south portal

(Right) Plan showing configuration of iconography on the south portal

1 Our Lady of the Three Kings
2 Prince Henry
3 The Archangel Michael
4 Portuguese coat of arms
5 and 6 Scenes from the life of St Jerome
7 St Jerome
8 St Augustin
9 St Gregory the Great
10 St Ambrose
11 St Catherine
12 St Appollonia
13 St Anastasia
14 St Lucy
15 The Prophet Daniel
16 The Prophet Ezekiel
17 The Prophet Jeremiah
18 The Prophet Isaiah
19 The Apostle Peter
20 The Apostle Paul
21–30 Apostles
31–36 Angels with instruments
37 St Sebastian
38 Medallion (Queen Maria?)
39 Medallion (King Manuel?)
40 Two lions' heads

respectively. They reveal how often the south portal, like cathedral portals in other towns and cities, was a meeting-place for members of the various craft guilds and sometimes served as the venue for ceremonial events. These signs almost always consist of a figure 4, or perhaps it is a draughtsman's set square. Halfway up the foot of the 4 are the initials, or an abbreviation, of the name of the guild member, with a pair of X's set across one another, or perhaps two compasses intertwined. This was a personal form of identification that could not be used by anyone else. Moreover, it could only be used by a man who had completed his apprenticeship and been accepted as a 'comrade', hence the almost secretive, 'Masonic' nature of the sign. The insignias here at Belém may belong to the master stonemasons who worked on the second stage of construction or to other craft guilds active in the city.

THE WEST PORTAL

The iconography of the west portal of the monastery picks up on the themes depicted on the south portal. Here the imagery concentrates more on the theological bases of Christian mythology surrounding Bethlehem, both the little town on the banks of the Tagus and the 'symbolic' one in the Bible. In three niches at the top of the arch are a series of sculptures dealing with the birth of the Messiah: the Mysteries of the Incarnation of Christ, the Nativity and the Adoration of the Magi. The scene in the stable at Bethlehem is at the central point, which is also the highest.

Statues of the royal founders, accompanied by their respective patron saints – King Manuel with St Jerome and his second wife, Queen Maria, with St John the Baptist – appear halfway up the portal on either side of the entrance, marking their presence here both in their public capacity and as private worshippers. Damião de Góis tells us that, at this door, 'the king commanded that an image of himself kneeling on a hassock, covered with flowing garments, be placed on one side; and on the other side his wife Maria also kneeling on a hassock. These two images are carved in lime-stone and the faces are quite lifelike'. They are, in fact, actual portraits, in the tradition of family mausoleums such as those at Champmol and Brou in Burgundy, where the founders of the house appear in an attitude of prayer or adoration. Such images also appear on monumental tombs like those sculpted by Gil de Siloe, including the late fifteenth-century statues of the Spanish Infante Alfonso and Juan de Padilla, dating from between 1500 and 1505, which are both at the Carthusian monastery of Miraflores in Burgos. Interestingly, the attitude of the king and queen mirrors that of the small figures of Joseph and Mary kneeling in adoration of the Infant Jesus in the niche above the door – another reference to the church's patron saint.

The remaining images have proved difficult to interpret, whether we rely on the chroniclers or on the principles of iconography. The most satisfactory interpretation would seem to be one of parallels and what art historians call 'typological opposition', in which Old Testament 'types' or figures are represented with – but subordinate to – New Testament 'antitypes'. On the right hand side, below King Manuel, we see St John the Evangelist and St Luke. St Matthew and St Mark are on the left. In other words, we have the Four Evangelists, who are absent from the south portal. Lower down are the Blessed Fernando, Henry the Navigator's younger brother, and St Vincent with a galleon. This is a harmonious pairing since both saints have local connections. The Blessed Fernando was associated with Portugal's recent triumphant history while St Vincent is the patron saint of Lisbon. On each buttress there are six smaller figures, thought to be the Twelve Apostles, who do not quite fit into the iconography scheme, since they already appear on the south portal. While it is easy to explain the presence, in a prominent position on the most exposed surface of the buttress, of St Paul and St Peter with their respective attributes, the other Apostles may possibly be part of another, more 'open-ended' narrative. On the right are believed to be St James and another saint, whose dilapidated condition makes identification impossible; both are set symmetrically against Moses, carrying the Tablets of the Law and Aaron, with priestly insignia, on the right. Again, this is a possible instance of type and antitype.

A different artistic language was used to create the west portal. Nicolau Chanterêne, who was commissioned to undertake the work on 2 January 1517, introduced a Classical vocabulary, and the statues he and his artisans produced were clearly guided by Renaissance aesthetics. The same applies to much of the ornamentation on the portal. While still resorting to Manueline iconography and a Manueline depressed arch, the sculptor's designs were clearly influenced by plainer, more harmonious, and better-proportioned architecture 'in the Roman style'.

Nicolau Chaterêne – the same 'Master Nicolao the Frenchman, the great sculptor' mentioned in the seventeenth century by Duarte Nunes de Leão as the creator of the altarpiece at the Mosteiro da Pena at Sintra – is believed to have been born in France and to have learnt his craft in Normandy. According to Rafael Moreira, he may well have worked in Rouen and Gaillon. By 1511 he was in Santiago de Compostela, where he was responsible for the sculptures on the pillars of the city's Royal Hospital. He turned up in Belém in 1517. The list of payments due to workers on the monastery site states: 'Master Nicolau, contractor for the main portal will bring eleven artisans and will receive twenty *milreis* per month.' His fame took him to Évora and to Coimbra, where he sculpted the famous pulpit in the church of Santa Cruz and some of the statues on the portal. The tombs of Kings Afonso I and Sancho I, the retablo in the Chapel of São Pedro in the city's Sé Velha (Old Cathedral) and the main altarpiece of the nearby Church of São Marcos are only some his achievements in Coimbra. They set the standard for future generations of artists. At that time, Évora and Coimbra were Portugal's leading centres of Renaissance sculpture; Évora because it had

(Above) View of the west portal (Nicolau Chanterêne, 1517)

(Right) West portal: Nativity scene above the door

West portal:
Annunciation

West portal: Virgin and
Child with St Joseph

easy access to the magnificent marble of the Alentejo region; Coimbra because it was the traditional base for sculptors working in the malleable white limestone known as 'Ançã stone', after the nearby village where it was quarried. It is obvious from the number of commissions Chanterêne received from Manuel I and John III that both monarchs thought highly of him. In the words of Pedro Dias, he was 'a real Renaissance artist, a man of culture, an intellectual'. He was also involved with Évora's humanist circles, which caused him frequent problems with the Inquisition. He was knighted by John III in 1526 and, ten years later, was honoured with the title of 'herald and carver of works in stone' with suitably generous remuneration. He held the post until 1551 when he retired, but not before bringing Portuguese art and architecture firmly into line with the principles of the Classical, 'Roman' style.

One of the most unusual features of the monastery complex would have been the 100-metre-long arcade running from east to west. From various pictures of the Jerónimos prior to the nineteenth-century restorations, it was a blind arcade. The structure would have been completed by 1516. A temporary and rather rough-and-ready roof would have been added later. There was space for pedestrians and carriages to access any part of the arcade. Above it was a large roofed structure with windows at more or less regular intervals, which was later converted into a dormitory. It was certainly an extraordinary building whose purpose is uncertain. According to the chronicles, King Manuel wanted to turn it into a kind of commercial centre or warehouse where goods from India were landed and business transacted. This never happened, and the ground floor was later enclosed and used by the monks to create pantries, storerooms and other practical facilities. The rest of the block was leased to tenants from outside the monastery.

Pedro Dias advances a credible hypothesis that King Manuel wanted to build a *paço* (royal residence) above the arcade, with direct links to the monastery, an idea that seems to comply closely with the principles of 'functionality' observed by Manueline architects. Examples of these principles can be seen in the Galeria das Damas (ladies' gallery), the ground floor arcade at the Paço Real at Évora. There were further instances at the Paço da Ribeira, which was destroyed in the Lisbon earthquake. The latter is depicted in an illuminated illustration in the king's *Book of Hours*. A similar illustration in the copy of Duarte Galvão's *Crónica de D. Afonso Henriques*, now in the Museu Conde Castro Guimarães, Cascais, shows an uninterrupted arcade at ground level. Arcades

Statue of Queen Maria
on the west portal

of this type also featured on other buildings in Lisbon, like the Hospital Real de Todos os Santos, and early industrial premises overlooking the Tagus.

The Belém arcade probably followed a sixteenth-century, late Gothic, architectural tradition of designing urban buildings that combined practicalities like ease of circulation, security and storage space with ostentatious display. The beauty of the Mosteiro dos Jerónimos and its harmony with its surroundings lies not so much in the quality of the materials used but in its eloquence as a monument.

Another factor that would have governed the creation of the arcade was its processional, devotional and liturgical function. There is no other explanation as to why images of the king and queen should have been carved on the west portal, right at the door of the vast portico, which must have been designed for a ceremonial purpose. Gradually, the gallery fell into a state of neglect until it was finally abandoned. Significantly, in 1551, when the body of King Manuel was brought for burial in the 'old church' (the old Belém chapel that still survived), the funeral cortège solemnly moved through the entire 'portico'. 'The entire portico, from the old church to the outer wall was empty, and the procession passed through it, entering through the main door of the church.'

View of the interior of
the church, seen from
half way along the
chancel

THE CHURCH

THE NAVES

The church at Belém is truly monumental. Designed as a hall-church, it has six free-standing pillars, three for each nave, plus two more forming part of the structure of the upper choir. The pillars are lavishly decorated with Plateresque grotesques, a concession to the classical, 'Iberian' taste, which tended to crop up in unexpected places during construction after João de Castilho took over.

Castilho built the vaulted ceiling above the naves. It was a daring technical innovation, never previously seen in Portugal. Firstly, it covered a vast space and, secondly, the Spanish architect was trying out a novel solution, both in the use of such extraordinarily slender ribs and in their configuration. The rib vaulting does not form the usual florid star shapes. The architect opted instead for net vaulting, springing from the 'palm tree' tops of the pillars and extending into liernes (non-structural short ribs) and tiercerons (intermediate ribs) to form eight-point intersections. The columns are linked together by gently curving ribs.

More innovative still are the differing shapes of the arches leading from the choir to the transept. The arch above the central nave describes a perfect semicircle, while those above the side naves are keel arches. The linking of the pillars by the net vaulting enabled the architect to build the roof in one continuous piece, with the tops of the columns or brackets converging to form a perfectly flat surface.

The vaulting above the transept, probably completed in 1522, is equally ambitious, with a slightly segmental profile. The whole structure is dictated by two supporting arches linking the pillars to the east wall. The supporting arches are also segmental. Three are buttressed by the north and south wall, three by the east wall. The tiercerons and the liernes create an uninterrupted, homogenous whole against which we can see a succession of straight ribs extending from wall to wall, and secured by bosses. This system divides the ceiling into four rectangular sections, inside which the tiercerons and liernes form a four-pointed star with a central lozenge. Each set of ribs is secured by a boss. Seven of the bosses are surrounded by circular ribs, which add to the overall, flattened effect of the ceiling. This is the most complex example of rib-vaulting in Portugal, described by George Kubler as 'the most accomplished realization of late-medieval ambitions to cover the largest possible space with the minimum support'. The ceiling covers a unified space of nearly twenty-nine metres long (north to south), twenty metres wide (east to west), and twenty-five metres high, creating the Iberian Peninsula's only 'cubic' space of its kind. Like the nave, the space is one and a half times as long as it is wide.

The lateral and central naves form a single unified space to accommodate the congregation. Viewed from the choir, the ceiling above the naves present a surprisingly 'Gothic' elevation contrasting to the much flatter vaulting. The elaborate interplay of shape and volume is one of the characteristics that make the ceiling so original.

Also noteworthy, especially on the north wall, is the rhythmic arrangement of the layers of stone blocks, which must have corresponded to the different stages of building the wall. The thinnest layers are interspersed with thicker, heavier ones, evidence of the meticulous planning of the building and the structural precision of its design. The final section of the wall on the level of the windows is built of smaller stones, in order to accommodate the complex system of roof supports.

We can glean some idea of the processes involved in deciding on and cutting the size of stones for use in construction, from the remains of craftsmen's 'sketches' on the north wall of the nave, next to the transept. Although they are so indistinct and easy to miss, the drawings are among the most important pieces of evidence of this kind to be found in Portugal. They appear on the vertical surface of what was probably the wall of the Castilian 'company's' workshop.

The sketches on the wall, which served as a model for making templates, include two concentric circles with lines radiating from the centre. This seems to be a design for an *œil de bœuf* or rose window, which would have enabled the craftsmen to manufacture the elements of the window on a scale of 1:1. There are also outlines of a piece of balustrade, with a pearl motif in the middle of the shaft and an interesting outline of half a tracery arch with concentric rosettes, similar to those used to decorate the arches in the cloister. This collection of drawings would have been used in conjunction with a finer 'grid' of drawings that helped determine the correct scale of each element. As some of them are high up on the wall we can assume either that the floor of the nave was originally higher than the finished one, or that there was scaffolding (or even a hut) against the wall.

View of the interior of the church, seen from below the upper choir

(Right) View of the church, with the ceiling above the crossing in the foreground

(Following pages) Ceiling above the crossing

Detail of craftsmen's sketches from the Manueline period on the north wall of the church

Medallion with a portrait of King Manuel on the north-east pillar of the church, next to the crossing

Among the most curious features of the church's interior are the twelve doors leading to the south-facing confessionals. The monks hearing confessions entered by twelve corresponding doors off the cloister. The confessionals are built in two adjoining compartments cut into the wall. These small, adjoining, intercommunicating spaces, described by George Kubler as 'membranous', are an example of one of the most interesting constants of sixteenth-century Portuguese architecture: its close connections with military architecture, which often inspired the basic structure of a building. Above the confessionals, inside the same thick wall from which they were hewn, runs a wide vaulted corridor giving access to the upper choir.

The church was also the setting for an opulent display of regal power, which has since disappeared. The dimensions and content of the iconography would have been governed by the requirement to eulogize and glorify the monarch.

Examples of the way in which the king was exalted by public orators and the romanticized accounts of royal feats can be seen from fictionalized chronicles such João de Barros's *Crónica do Imperador Clarimundo* (*c*.1520), or the prologue and the narrative of *A Crónica de D. Afonso Henriques* by Duarte Galvão (written before 1517). Both highlight the association of national destiny with the Miracle of Ourique, which sanctified the Portuguese coat of arms. On the eve of the Battle of Ourique (1139), King Afonso Henriques saw a vision of the Crucifixion. In the ensuing battle he defeated five Moorish kings and adopted their five shields as his coat of arms, incorporating the five wounds of Christ to commemorate his miraculous encounter. These examples show that inscriptions such as *In Hoc Signo Vinces* (In this sign conquer), the motto of the first Christian Roman Emperor, Constantine – next to the Crucifixion in the chancel of the church of Santa Cruz in Coimbra or on those on coins issued by the king – are based on a well-founded 'myth of origins'.

The iconography in the Jeronimos church would have been chosen to pay tribute to and sanctify the king. This is why some 130 unfilled and unadorned niches were incorporated into the architectural supports. Their exact purpose remains a mystery but Rafael Moreira suggests that the niches were 'perhaps intended for vigilant effigies of members of the Portuguese royal family, the seventeen rulers beginning with Henry of Burgundy, or their patron saints. The display here of an 'ancestors' gallery' and their insignias points to the sacred and paternalistic nature of the royal lineage.' To support his theory, Moreira cites the examples of San Juan de Los Reyes in Toledo, the Emperor Maximilian's tomb at Innsbruck, Westminster Abbey and the chapel of King's College, Cambridge. These and other arguments suggest that the church was intended as a national monument, where a procession of monarchs kept a stern and watchful eye on political and diplomatic manoeuvrings.

As well as hazarding guesses about secular images, we can also make some assumptions about sacred ones. The Twelve Apostles above the twelve confessionals and the Four Evangelists in the niches above the transept are arranged in a logical sequence. The remaining niches are similarly occupied, but in no particular order. Perhaps, with some of them filled, logic broke down in the interests of getting the job done. As Rafael Moreira claims, the transept was 'not a space for processions but a meeting point and hence a holy place in which rituals of state were performed, deliberately designed to serve as a backdrop to the various acts involving the monarch in his role as mediator between the life of the nation and the sphere of the divine; from liturgical celebrations to civic occasions and funerals'.

If we accept this quite reasonable argument, we might assume that the medallion, showing a finely-executed profile of a person identified as the master builder in charge of the project – some say it is Boitaca, others, João de Castilho – does, in fact, bear the image of King Manuel. The portrait has the monarch's characteristic features and occupies a privileged position on a pillar on the north side of the church, facing the chancel, close to the place where, under the terms of his will, the king would be buried. Although it was only in 1522 that João de Castilho finished building the church, the architect would have taken account of the monarch's wishes.

It is also likely that the way space was organized in the Jeronimite's church was a response to new ecclesiastical policy introduced before the Reformation. Provision of a unified space for worship was one of the essential requirements of pre-Reformation thinking, which claimed the existence of a huge, united congregation that would come and worship in vast naves such as this. The worshipers would throng into the immense space, humbled by the awesome presence of Christ, symbolized by the chancel (which at this point would have been Boitaca's original structure). In the gloom of the transept, the chancel would have been an even more resplendent focal point, a clear reference to the king's absolute and overruling power.

THE CHOIR

The choir was completed somewhat later than the rest of the church and was adapted to fit into the existing structure. It too was restored following the earthquake of 1755.

In the lower choir, at ground level next to the west door, are two chapels: the Chapel of St Leonard is on the right and the Chapel of the Way of the Cross is on the left. This chapel was formerly dedicated to St Anthony, because it was the headquarters of the brotherhood of that name. It is literally packed with glorious gold carvings, dating from 1669. It also contains four fifteenth-century tapestries depicting scenes from Christ's Passion, in early Portuguese baroque style. The other chapel, its walls now bare, contains a baptismal font, a collection of reliquaries and an exquisite Italian faience image of St Anthony, once venerated in the chapel opposite. In 1940 the tombs of Vasco da Gama and Luís de Camões were moved here. Both were sculpted in 1894 by Costa Mota Tio in 'reproduction', neo-Manueline style, typical expressions of the aesthetics of the nineteenth-century restorers. The presence of the two great men transformed the church into a great patriotic shrine and a symbolic, albeit unofficial, national pantheon.

The remarkable choir stalls, flanked by two tower-like structures, are the highlight of the upper choir. This is Portugal's most important example of Renaissance woodcarving. Rafael Moreira's research has proved beyond doubt that the choir stalls were designed by Diogo de Torralva and were built around 1550 by the Spaniard Diego de Zarza, possibly in collaboration with the Flemish woodcarver Philippe de Vries.

The present configuration consists of sixty stalls arranged in two rows: upper and lower. The seats, with their misericords and their exceptionally high backs, are built of chestnut and Flanders oak. There were originally eighty-four stalls, before a part of the side elevations was dismantled and removed. The lower row is decorated with reliefs of secular motifs – ships, festivals, comic figures – interspersed with small figures of Atlas and other obviously Flemish-inspired motifs; these were based on contemporary engravings from Antwerp, which were then in circulation in Portugal. On the upper row, busts in the 'classical' style alternate with figures of saints. The choir has extraordinary dignity. The degree of craftsmanship in the woodcarving combines with the projecting pilasters to give the whole structure an 'architectural' feel, ranking alongside the works of the finest artists in Europe. With its blend of High Renaissance vocabulary and flashes of inspired imagination, it already shows Mannerist tendencies. The baroque paintings of the Apostles are the work of a run-of-the-mill artisan and of only minor interest. On the balustrade, restored in the nineteenth century, when the original collapsed after the earthquake, is a monumental image of Christ Crucified, given to the monastery in 1551 by King Manuel's son, Prince Luís. It was a particular favourite of King Philip I of Spain, who was impressed by its dramatic realism. The uniquely expressive, polychrome wood image, the work of the Flemish artist Phillipe de Vries, was also a precursor of Mannerism.

Chapel of the Way of the Cross

Tomb of Vasco da Gama
(Costa Mota Tio, 1894)

(Right) Tomb of Luís de
Camões (Costa Mota
Tio, 1894)

View of the south side
of the upper choir,
with choir stalls

View of the north side
of the upper choir,
with choir stalls

(Above left) Detail of
choir stall (Diogo de
Torralva, Diogo de
Zarza,
1550–51)

(Left) Detail of a choir
stall

(Right) *Christ Crucified*
(Philippe de Vries, 1551)

THE CHANCEL

The present chancel was commissioned by John III's widow, Queen Catarina, who acted as regent for the infant King Sebastian from 1557 until 1562.

The original chancel, built in the reign of King Manuel, was planned as the king's personal mausoleum. Manuel's mortal remains were brought there and buried in a simple grave on the orders of his son, John III. When the bodies of Manuel's second wife, Maria, and John III were also laid to rest there, the Manueline chancel's original role as the place where the king would lie in solitary state was quickly forgotten.

At the same time, the political situation in Portugal led Catarina to assume a much more decisive role in affairs of state, and her increased status was reflected in a more assertive style of architecture, of which the Mosteiro dos Jerónimos would be one of the most obvious examples. Plans for a new chancel, which would eventually become the final resting place of the kings and queens of the imperial dynasty of Avis-Beja, began to take shape. Jerónimo de Ruão was commissioned to draw up the plans. He was inspired by highly innovative aesthetic principles: Classical, but interpreted in a way that can only be described as Mannerist. Ruão's ideas would have been seen as revolutionary, marking as they did a dramatic move away from the Manueline style of the rest of the building. Today, we can only imagine the bitter controversy they would have caused at the time.

The first section of the chancel has a rectangular ground plan, the second section is semicircular. The concave wall behind the high altar continues upwards into a hemispherical dome, which joins the barrel vault of the stone-coffered ceiling. In the side walls are deep windows whose splayed arches, built according to the laws of perspective, echo the surrounding panelling. The far wall consists of a mesh of stone mouldings following the curve of the surface and framing the altarpiece. This once consisted of six altar panels; now only five remain.

Along the side walls are two rows of free-standing pillars; Ionic pillars on the lower level, Corinthian above. The spaces between the columns lead to the arcosolia – the vaulted stone chambers – containing the monumental tombs of King Manuel and Queen Maria, on the Gospel (or right) side, and King John III and Queen Catarina of the Epistle (or left) side. The expressions 'Gospel' and 'Epistle' side arise from the old tradition according to which the priest at Mass would stand on the right of the altar to read from the Gospels and in the left to read from the Epistles. The tombs have a Classical, pyramidal shape and each is supported by two marble elephants, in a composition clearly inspired by the mausoleums in the Malatesta Temple at Rimini, Italy. Each tomb bears a Latin inscription by the humanist André de Resende. This style of architecture, one of whose most avant-garde features was the contrasting use of white, blue and pink Alentejo marble, attracted considerable interest. One admirer was Philip II of Spain – who became Philip I of Portugal in 1580, and who commissioned the tombs. The outlines of tomb configuration, as well as the way in which the sculptor defines volume and surface, create a curious sensation of space itself being modelled in the manner of small-scale 'architecture' produced by other craftsmen such as gold- and silversmiths. The iconography in the chancel is very austere and it is the architecture itself that predominates, both in its use of the Classical orders and its perfect proportions. A further innovative touch was to make the brightly painted and dramatic retablo behind the high altar the only splash of colour in this sober space.

The retablo by Lourenço de Salzedo (1535–78) was completed between 1570 and 1572. According to the distinguished art historian Vítor Serrão, this is one of most impressive and mature manifestations of early Portuguese Mannerist painting. The altarpiece is arranged in two rows: the upper row consisting of three panels depicting scenes from Christ's Passion. In the centre is the Deposition, with Jesus carrying the Cross, and Jesus bound to the pillar on either side. Below them are two (formerly three) paintings with scenes from the Nativity and the Adoration of

View of the chancel (Jerónimo de Ruão, 1565?–72)

Tomb of King Manuel
(Jerónimo de Ruão,
1565?–72)

(Right) Altarpiece in the
chancel (Lourenço de
Salzedo, 1570–72)

(Far right) Sacrarium
(João de Sousa, 1674–8)

the Magi. The painting missing from the centre showed the Madonna and Child. Although the decorations in the chancel were added more than sixty years after the church's foundation, they still centred on themes relating to the patron saint. The iconography, its colours and the shape of the figures, reveal Salzedo as an artist attuned to the very latest tendencies in art, prepared to learn from the Italian school and produce work of the same *terribilità* (awesome grandeur) as Michelangelo, in complete contrast to the rather anodyne ceremoniousness of contemporary ecclesiastical art. The acid colours and huge human figures enhance the monumental splendour of the retablo, reinforcing its didactic message and capturing the mood prevailing in the Catholic Church in the early years of the Counter Reformation, following the Council of Trent. In the centre of the altar is a majestic baroque sacrarium made by the goldsmith João de Sousa between 1674 and 1678. The central panel of the retablo was removed when it was installed.

Because of the status of the Mosteiro dos Jerónimos as one of the Portuguese kingdom's great architectural and artistic showcases, it eventually housed the finest examples of late Gothic, Portuguese Renaissance and Mannerism. Here, too, the language and forms of the Classical revival were established, marking the end of an era in the nation's history. With the death of King Sebastian, the Avis-Beja dynasty came to an end, so too did the golden age of discovery. Work at Belém also came to a standstill.

The large transept contains a number of altars housed in large niches or aedicules, surrounded by entablatures whose relatively 'plain' Manueline decorations do not quite match other examples in the church, which suggests they are of a later date. The altars are dedicated to saints revered during the Counter Reformation, with those of Our Lady of Bethlehem and St Jerome on the north side, and those of St Paula and Our Lady, Star of the Sea on the south side. Those dedicated to St Eustachia and the Sacred Heart of Jesus are situated next to the large chapel in the south transept.

Covering a vast empty space, the ceiling was constructed with great technical sophistication at a moment that marked a turning point in Portuguese architecture. Two longitudinal supporting arches rest on the eastern wall of the transept and the first set of pillars in the nave. The segmental arched roof is supported by a network of ribs in a predominantly rectangular pattern. The bronze keystones, formerly painted with polychrome heraldic devices associated with Manuel I, such as the Cross of the Order of Christ, the armilliary sphere (a navigational instrument) and the royal coat of arms, are framed by curved ribs describing a perfect circle.

The ceiling of the side chapels is a semicircular vault. The chapels contain the tombs of the children of King Manuel on the Gospel side and descendants of John III on the Epistle side. The lintels of the wall panels are decorated with typically Mannerist stonework motifs, in the Flemish style. Jerónimo de Ruão probably designed them while busy working on the chancel and they are less 'experimental' than the rest of the building. The side walls of the chapels consist of an alternating series of altars and wall monuments. Among them is the tomb of the Cardinal-King Henry on the north side, while on the south side at the end of the chapel is the tomb of the young King Sebastian, killed at the Battle of Alcácer-Quibir in 1578. His body was never found and the sarcophagus contains the remains of an identified man.

A very strange phenomenon is reported to occur at the monastery at certain times of the year, when the sun's rays penetrate the church in an extraordinary way. Around the spring and autumn equinoxes the sun shines straight onto the silver sacrarium and seems to turn it to gold. This may be purely coincidental, although it is conceivable that the alignment of the dormitory, rose window and the body of the church was deliberate. This almost mystical event was reported by the chronicler Diogo de Jesus and corroborated by Jacinto de São Miguel. It was also described by the late Father Felicidade Alves, speaking with the authority of Belém's former parish priest and a devoted

student and historian of the monastery. According to Father Felicidade Alves, for twenty days before the spring equinox and between 28 October and the thirtieth day after the autumn equinox 'the sun's golden rays . . . from the hour of Vespers until sunset, entering from the east and covering a distance of 450 paces, pass in a straight line through the dormitory, choir and church to the sacrarium. The sun seems to be asking its Creator for leave of absence from such an illustrious monastery for the brief hours of the night, and promising to return again to shine at dawn.'

THE SACRISTY

Although hidden away in a discreet corner of the monastery, the sacristy is one of the monument's architectural jewels.

The pillar in the centre of this square space would have been seen as a remarkable structural innovation at the time it was built. The ribs springing from the pillar support the depressed vaulted ceiling. The configuration of the vaulting with its curved, bulging ribs resting on the twisted corbels of the engaged columns in the perimeter walls is very much like the fan vaulting seen in Great Britain. The central pillar is decorated with a series of Plateresque-style reliefs lending the clearly late-Gothic sacristy an air of Classical dignity.

Running along the walls is a sober arcade. Its uncluttered, austere design is attributed to Jerónimo de Ruão. On the back wall are fourteen paintings describing the life of St Jerome, attributed to Simão Rodrigues and dating from between 1600 and 1610. The remaining paintings displayed here would have come from other parts of the monastery. They include a series of six panels painted by António Campelo, presumably the ones that occupied the large aedicules in the cloister.

Detail of sacrarium door

THE CLOISTERS

LOWER STOREY

The entry to the cloisters is through what was once the main entrance to the monastery, a door situated in the recess between the west façade of the church and the dormitory block. It is a Classical structure, designed by Teodósio de Frias in 1625 and executed by the stonemason Diogo Vaz. Beside the door itself are two large busts of Hercules and Julius Caesar, framing a tablet bearing a Latin inscription composed by André de Resende. It reads: VASTA MOLE SACRUM DIVINAE IN LITTORE MATRI / REX POSUIT REGUS MAXIMUM EMMANUEL. / AUXIT OPUS HERES RFEGNI, ET PIETATIS, UTERQUE / SRTUCTURA CERTANT, RELIGIONE PARES, which translates as: 'King Manuel, the greatest of monarchs, built on the seashore / a vast and magnificent church dedicated to the Mother of God. / The heir to his kingdom and his piety continued his work / Equal in their faith, in this building each seeks to surpass the other'.

(Left) Main door of the chapter house (Rodrigo de Pontezilha, 1517–21)

View of the cloister (Diogo Boitaca, 1502–13; João de Castilho, c.1517–20)

95

Entrance hall of the monastery, leading to the cloister

(Opposite) A corner of the cloister showing the contrast between the façade of an already restored wing and a section of the adjacent wing before restoration in 2000–01

Beyond the ticket office, on the right of the staircase, is a modest corridor linking the entrance to the cloister. Passing from the small, busy space into an amazingly large, open area is an interesting experience.

When it was built, the cloister was absolutely unique. Nothing like it had ever been seen before. It is built on a square ground plan, its corners cut away to form what is virtually an octagon. The idea of building two storeys completely in stone was a major innovation and the lavish decoration on the upper storey marked a totally new aesthetic departure, showing the importance that was attached to the cloister.

The various stages of completion are not immediately obvious, especially on the lower floor, but a closer analysis reveals that the original design envisaged a much simpler decorative scheme. Boitaca drew up the plans for the cloister and carried out the initial work, including many of the late Gothic features that were his trademark, including cylindrical external pilasters and buttresses. When João de Castilho took over, work was already under way. The arcades, however, were unfinished, or at least only those on the east and west sides were complete. Aware of the kind of ornamentation and iconography demanded by his patron, Castilho updated the original plan by adding to the structure. He also covered Boitaca's original cylindrical pilasters with rectangular ones, decorating them with Plateresque-style reliefs. Some of the original pilasters and buttresses can still be seen on the upper storey of the cloister and give some idea of what Boitaca's cloister would have looked like.

However, the overall atmosphere and visual effect of the cloister with its opulent and eclectic ornamentation is distinctly Manueline. Most of the decorations in the arcades are plant motifs,

View of the cloister, the
north façade, prior to
the restoration works
of 2002

with some animal images and fantasy figures, and the walls seem to exude an exotic, magical air. The unexpected combination of late Gothic animal, plant and allegorical motifs with the more learned Lombard style of ornamentation, resulted in a piece of artistic and architectural creativity like no other.

Along the walls of the cloister is a series of medallions showing the Instruments of the Passion of Christ, and Portuguese heraldic devices from the time of Manuel I. These are followed by reliefs of scenes from the life of Christ – the Annunciation, the Flagellation (or Christ bound to the pillar), the Pietà and a Vision of St Jerome.

Moving clockwise from the entrance to the cloister, on the corner of the west wing is the Portuguese coat of arms, followed by medallions showing an unusual Cross of St Andrew, which is also the X standing for the name of Christ; the whip with which Christ was scourged and the spear with which he was pierced on the Cross; the Five Wounds; the Crown of Thorns; a Cross set on a globe, symbolizing Christendom, and finally, on a moulding, the Flagellation of Christ. Another moulding on the north wing shows a relief of the 'Pietà', followed by five more medallions: the Five Wounds, a bunch of white lilies (emblem of Queen Maria); a letter 'M' topped with a crown (which could refer to King Manuel, Queen Maria or the Virgin Mary) and the letters IHS, the Greek monogram for the name of Jesus. This wing ends with a relief representing the Annunciation. The east wing contains a relief of the Vision of St Jerome, followed by the pillar and the rope (references to the Flagellation), a Cross with thorns and a rose (a symbol which many esoterists see as a forerunner of Rosicrucianism), the ladder; the pincers, the hammer, the nails and the whip; a cockerel (symbolizing Peter's denial of Christ) and finally the coat of arms of Queen Maria. The south wing features the Avis coat of arms, and four medallions with images that some claim are portraits of the Portuguese navigators, Pedro Álvares Cabral, Nicolau Coelho, Vasco da Gama and Paulo da Gama, and finally a medallion showing a sunburst.

There appear to be two ways of interpreting the imagery in the cloister: one religious and the other secular.

On the north façade are tablets bearing symbols of the monarchy: the armilliary sphere, King Manuel's emblem, and the lilies, emblem of his second wife Queen Maria. Next to them are essentially Christian symbols: IHS (the Greek monogram of the name of Jesus), the crowned M (Virgin

Relief in the south-east corner of the cloister: the Portuguese coat of arms supported by dragons

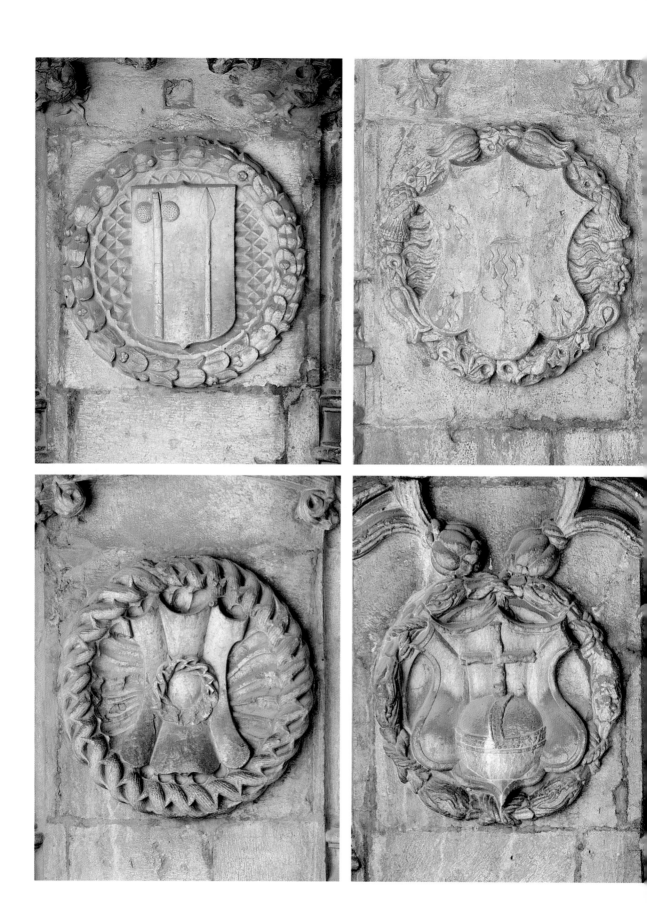

(Opposite top left)
The spear, scourge and sponge filled with vinegar and hyssop

(Opposite top right)
The Five Wounds of Christ

(Opposite left)
The Crown of Thorns

(Opposite right)
The Globe and Cross: symbol of Christendom

(Above) Relief in the north-east corner of the cloister: Christ bound to the pillar

(Left) Relief in the corner of the cloister: the Pietà

Relief of the Annunciation in the corner of the cloister

Mary, Maria Regina) and the Five Wounds. This time they express the mythical connection between Jesus – Immanuel – and the king, and between the Virgin Mary and Queen Maria. It is patently obvious that His Majesty believed that his name shaped his destiny. It was the same name as the infant Immanuel who Isaiah prophesied (Isaiah 7: 10–14) would be born of a virgin, a sign that Jerusalem would be set free – the prophecy that St Matthew interpreted as predicting the birth of Jesus (Matthew 1: 23). Contemporary chroniclers and others who wrote eulogistically about the monarch made much of this comparison, associating it with the divine right of kings, a frequent topic in their writings.

(Top left) Medallion and plaque showing the Five Wounds

(Top right) The emblem of Queen Maria: a bunch of daisies or white lilies (also the symbol of the Virgin Mary)

Medallion in the north wing: the letter 'M' may stand for Manuel, Maria (the Queen) or Mary the Virgin

(Top left) The armillary sphere, emblem of King Manuel, with the royal crown. The inscription reads: I. EMANVEL R.P. ET ALG. V. (Manuel I King of Portugal and the Algarves)

(Top right) Plaque with the symbol IHS (the Greek monogram for the name of Jesus)

Pillar of the Flagellation and the rope with which Christ was bound

Crown of Thorns and Cross inscribed on a rose. Scholars of traditional sciences believe this to be one of the first Rosicrucian symbols, which in turn forms the basis of the mythology connecting the Discoverers with the Knights Templars. What is certain is that the iconography in the Belém cloister draws on the special symbols of the Society of Jesus, specifically the conscious and constant association with the rose (such as Mystical Rose, one of the Litanies of the Virgin) the sunburst (symbol of Christ), the Cross and the Greek monogram for the name of Jesus (IHS)

(Top left) Relief showing 'St Jerome, penitent'

(Top right) Medallion in the west wing: the ladder, hammer and pincers, Instruments of the Passion of Christ. This provides an interesting 'semantic key' to the symbolism of the cloister, containing the description of the instruments used to nail Christ to the Cross, as well as those used to bring him down before he was laid in the tomb

(Above left) Three nails and the whip

(Above right) The cock, a symbol taken from the New Testament story of Peter's betrayal but which also symbolizes dawn (and hence the Resurrection). Moving clockwise around the south wing, the cock precedes the sun symbol

The south-east corner of the cloister: the emblem of Queen Maria, surmounted by the Cross of Christ

(Opposite, above) Coat of arms of the House of Avis

(Opposite, below) Coat of arms of Queen Maria

On the south façade we see the four busts sometimes identified as four navigators but which this writer prefers to interpret as four grandees of Antiquity; great emperors or generals like Alexander, Scipio, Caesar or Augustus, often cited in texts extolling imperialist virtues. They might also be mythical heroes of similar stature, such as Hercules. Beyond them is the representation of the sun and in the corners, the coats of arms of the king and queen of Portugal, which seem to mark the physical and human boundaries of their empire. On this side of the cloister there is hardly any strictly religious symbolism. Here, the imagery serves a secular or temporal purpose and is a tribute to human achievement.

If we interpret the imagery on the north side of the cloister as the 'Christian cycle', focusing on Jesus and Mary and the divinity of the monarchy, that on the south side can be seen as the 'heroic cycle' devoted to human and national exploits. Then, if we look at the parallels in the two iconographies, we know we are witnessing the intersection of the history of Portugal and the known world, and the history of Christianity. The sovereign assumes an intermediary role between the two that is both apostolic and heroic. Christianity and its traditions are in themselves the most powerful expression of the glory of the empire and its ruler King Manuel.

The four busts could also allude to the 'four pagan empires' that Daniel prophesied. These were the Babylonian, Persian, Greek and Roman Empires. The 'fifth empire' would be the Kingdom of God with Christ at its head – a concept with which Portugal strongly identified during the age of discovery. The fifth medallion with the abstract image of the sun with its twelve rays, represented both the *sol justitiae*, namely Christ 'the sun of righteousness' and the 'fifth empire'.

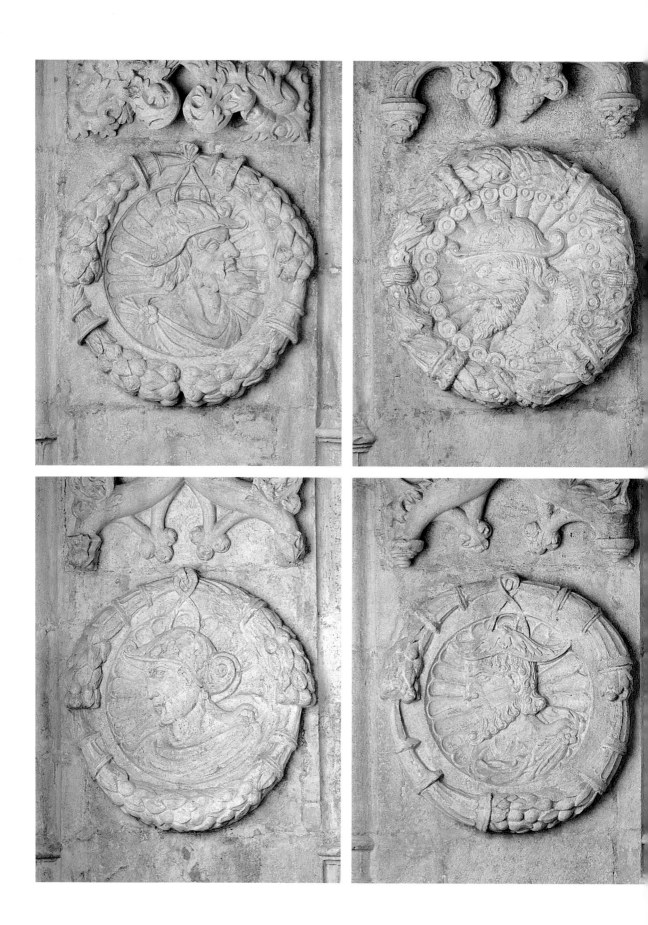

(Opposite, far left) Bust in relief (possibly Pedro Álvares Cabral)

(Opposite, left) Bust in relief (possibly Nicolau Coelho)

(Opposite, below, far left) Bust in relief (possibly Paulo da Gama)

(Opposite, below left) Bust in relief (possibly Vasco da Gama)

(Right) Medallion in the south wing: the sun with twelve rays or *Sol Justitiae*. It is thought to represent the foundation of the Fifth Empire, but is also a metaphor for the Risen Christ, placed on the south side and traditionally associated with the idea of light

Cultural and religious factors would also have contributed to the content of this fascinating visual imagery scheme. At the time the monastery was built, Portugal was living through the period leading up to the Reformation. This was certainly the reason why King Manuel favoured the Jeronimites, conscious of the role the monks would play in revitalizing spirituality in the religious orders during the third decade of the sixteenth century. John II's widow, Leonor, and her court had quietly supported the new ideas coming from northern Europe and Italy, from Erasmian humanism to Flemish mysticism, by way of the austere spirituality of Savonarola. The court was already under the literary influence of Ludolpho of Saxony's *Vita Christi*, a book that played a vital role in the consolidation of Christocentrism, a school of thought that put Christ at the centre of Christian morality. On Leonor's instructions, it was translated into Portuguese by the Cistercian monks of Alcobaça in 1495. The ideas expressed in another contemporary publication, *Boosco Deleitoso*, proposed that the exemplary Christian life was that of the ascetic and hermit – very much in line with Jeronimite thinking – and aroused great interest in court circles. The 'old queen' Leonor, the king's sister, was involved in getting this book published in Portugal.

Consequently, the cloister's religious iconography is based on imagery introduced by the northern European *devotio moderna* (or 'modern devotion') movement that revolved around the humanity of Christ and stressed the importance of the inner life. Viewed in this light, the framed reliefs in the corners of the cloister and the paintings that once occupied the large rectangular aedicules take on added meaning, beyond the *via crucis* represented by the more abstract medallions. They help us understand the aspirations of the sixteenth-century Portuguese élite to lead ethical, moral and spiritual lives and to achieve mystical union with Christ through the redemptive power of his sufferings. They used visual clues such as these to create a contemplative mood. All this in preparation for the *via unitiva* – the ultimate state of intimacy with God. Images like the Instruments of the Passion and other Christian symbols, such as the globe, IHS, first used by the Franciscans, and the Five Wounds of Christ define this as a place of contemplation, and of both 'physical' and interior pilgrimage.

Other sources may have influenced the iconographic scheme. For example, in his *Auto da Alma* (The Soul's Journey), the Portuguese dramatist Gil Vicente presents a version of the parable of the Good Samaritan, in which the leading players are the Human Soul, the Devil and the Guardian Angel. On his journey, the Soul is welcomed by the Doctors of the Church, Saints Augustine, Jerome, Ambrose and Thomas to an 'inn' (the Church) where he is served with 'delicacies' – the Instruments of the Passion of Christ. The cloister may have been constructed and decorated slightly before the play was written, but this does not mean that the allegory of the Church as an inn and the Instruments of the Passion as food was not widely known, and could have provided inspiration for the decoration of the Jeronimite cloister. Interestingly, in the *Auto* St Jerome is one of the saints offering the delicacies – the whip, the crown of thorns and the nails. King Manuel and the old Queen Leonor attended a performance of the play at the Paço da Ribeira during Holy Week in 1518. Gil Vicente himself probably directed the play and designed the scenery. The visual imagery of the drama matches that of the medallions. The playwright's stage directions state:

> St Jerome presents the delicacies. The delicacies referred to in this scene are the whips which are taken from the platters and presented at the table, whereupon the Doctor Saints kneel and sing *Ave flagellum;* . . . The second delicacy is the crown of thorns and in this scene they are taken from the platters and the Doctor Saints kneel and sing *Ave corona espiniarum.* . . . And in this scene Saint Augustine presents the nails and all kneel in adoration, singing *Dulce lignum, dulcis clavus.*

The number of Instruments of the Passion seen here is typical of the transitional period between the Middle Ages and the Renaissance. From the thirteenth century onwards, six instruments were usually represented, while there are ten in the cloister at Belém, in line with the Europe-wide tendency in the fifteenth century to extend the motif to include the cock that crowed at Peter's denial, the hammer, the nails and the pincers. Here, as some of the inscriptions suggest, they also fill their traditional role of 'Christ's coat of arms'.

Among the rooms around the cloister, the refectory with its depressed ribbed ceiling is outstanding for its harmonious design and the quality of the architecture. It was the work of the master builder Leonardo Vaz. Beneath the low moulded cornice running all along the walls, the rich colours of the rococo *azulejos* creates a truly Portuguese atmosphere. This is a typical example of Portuguese architects' skill in combining materials and form to striking effect, while still obeying a long-standing tradition. At the end of the refectory in a niche is a painting of St Jerome in his study, from the time of John IV, attributed to the court painter Avelar Rebelo. Nothing remains of the kitchen, guest house and granary, which were integrated into the perimeter walls of the building when the monastery was handed over to the Casa Pia in the nineteenth century. They were sacrificed to make way for inferior structures, as were other rooms on the first floor, including the famous library, now used as exhibition space.

The chapter house in the west wing was left unfinished in the sixteenth century and was only completed during the nineteenth-century restorations. The fine twin doors divided by a trumeau were constructed between 1517 and 1518 by the stonemason Rodrigo de Pontezilha, one of Castilho's team of artisans, with the help of the young André Pilarte who would later introduce the

Renaissance style to the Algarve region of southern Portugal. The doors are executed in early Renaissance style with Lombard ornamentation featuring festoons and candelabra. The outer side of the door is the work of the restorers, who attempted to 'imitate' the original. Inside the chapter house, we can clearly see where the architects in charge of restorations began their work. The wall had only been built to ceiling level. In 1886, builders added a neo-Manueline ceiling and finally a raised platform in the same style. The ceiling was designed by Raimundo Valadas and the decoration by Simões de Almeida, also responsible for the tomb of the eminent historian and mayor of Belém, Alexandre Herculano, who died in 1877. Herculano's tomb conforms to late nineteenth-century revivalist precepts and his burial here could be seen as his final just reward. Although only indirectly, he was instrumental in inventing the term 'Manueline' and was a passionate defender of Portugal's cultural heritage at a time when very few people either knew or cared about it.

UPPER STOREY

The upper story of the cloister is reached via two flights of a monumental staircase, leading from the entrance hall, which once provided access to the Sala dos Reis, or Room of the Kings. The original staircase in a sophisticated, Mannerist style was demolished in 1868, while the present one was built in accordance with some debatable notion of stylistic unity.

Rafael Moreira has deciphered the decorative scheme on the cloister's upper level. Although probably completed later than that on the ground floor, and despite its Plateresque tone, it harmonizes with the mythical and political themes that inspired the other cycles of Manueline iconography. Each arch is decorated with life-size religious, allegorical and secular statues: saints, virtues and historical figures, some of them hard to identify.

In the east wing are a martyred female saint and the allegories of Prudence and Charity, the figure of the Church, and the allegory of Faith. On the south side are an Evangelist (or Daniel), and the allegories of Fortitude, Temperance and Liberality. On the west side we find the allegory of Justice, the Prophet Isaiah, Manuel I, the allegory of Hope, and St Ursula. On the north side are St Margaret, a sybil, St Mary Magdalene, St Catherine and St Lucy.

It comes as no surprise to find King Manuel in the company of the Prophet Isaiah and the figure of hope, both of which had personal resonance for the monarch. He regarded his name as a direct reference to Isaiah's prophesy, while his emblem, the armillary sphere, was interpreted by contemporary chroniclers and heralds as a visual pun: *sphera do mondo* (the earth's sphere) and *spera do mondo* (the hope of the world).

What is most striking about the whole iconographic scheme is the powerful presence of the cardinal, theological and common virtues, with Faith, Charity and Prudence on the east side, together with the allegorical figure of the Church; Fortitude, Liberality and Temperance on the south side and Hope and Justice on the west. Such a systematic presentation of the virtues is unique in Portugal and is probably one of the most comprehensive of its kind anywhere. Similar representations of the virtues would appear later on the royal tombs at the church of Santa Cruz in Coimbra. It is also interesting that they are dedicated to the royal house and to King Manuel in particular, so that the ruler is inevitably associated with these qualities.

Ars memorativa (the 'art of memory'), an esoteric technique practised during the Renaissance, used both mnemonics and various other reference points with ethical connotations. For example, the figure of St Thomas always evoked the four virtues of Prudence, Justice, Fortitude and Temperance. In the mid-fourteenth century, a book entitled *Rosaio della Vita* proposed a list of vices and virtues and the physical form in which they should be represented in order to make them immediately recognizable.

(Left) Cloister: view of
the upper storey

(Top left) Martyred saint

(Top right) Allegory of
Prudence

Allegory of Charity

(Top left) Allegory of
Faith

(Top right) St Mary
Magdalene

St Catherine

(Top left) St Lucy

(Top right)
Unidentified figure
(possibly a sibyl)

The Prophet Isaiah

(Left) Allegory of Liberality

(Above right) King Manuel (?)

(Right) Allegory of Hope

(Top left) Allegory of
Temperance

(Left) St Ursula (?)

(Right) St Margaret

(Above) Bosses in the vaulted ceiling of the cloister opposite the chapter house: the sun and in the foreground, a plaque with the inscription: *El-Rey* (The King)

Boss in the vaulted ceiling of the cloister: St James

Decorative detail:
the 'hand'

Future research will doubtless reveal more, but we can be certain that the imagery at the Mosteiro dos Jerónimos was part of a cultural practice based on the rules of rhetoric and the use of mnemonics to deliver a message that was particularly relevant in King Manuel's era. At the same time, it brought together a compendium of worldly knowledge, and divine and regal power. It also intensified the effect of architecture that was all about grandeur, proclaiming the might of the sovereign, his realm and his God.

The rich symbolism of the decorations in the cloister of the Jeronimite monastery and on the south portal has engendered a series of esoteric interpretations and fascinating speculation such as that found in the scholarly and compelling writings of the mysterious twentieth-century alchemist Falcanelli. In the 1920s, his book *Le Mystère des Cathédrales*, translated in the 1970s as *The Mystery of the Cathedrals*, claimed that the secrets of alchemy were openly displayed on the walls of Gothic cathedrals. Another outstanding contribution to the debate comes from António Telmo with his intelligent and inspiring reading of the 'secret' history and destiny of Portugal as prophetically inscribed in the stones of the cloister.

However, we must be cautious and concentrate on what is known and not on any extra dimension, other than the unexpected and poetic magic that the Mosteiro dos Jerónimos truly does possess. The experience of visiting the monastery can be enriched even further by reading its messages in conjunction with *Mensagem*, the enigmatic cycle of poems by Fernando Pessoa, who was photographed here.

BIBLIOGRAPHY

This text is the result of a reworking of a number of essays by the author on the architecture and symbolism of the Mosteiro dos Jerónimos which are listed in the bibliography. Since the bibliography is so rich and extensive we should like to make special mention of the contributions of several scholars, particularly those of Francisco Adolfo Varnhagen in the mid-nineteenth century, and Reinaldo dos Santos, Virgílio Correia and João Barreira, in the mid-twentieth century. We should like also to honour the memory of Father José da Felicidade Alves and pay tribute to his tireless efforts in compiling and classifying information about the monastery. More recently, Rafael Moreira has produced some invaluable work, from which much of the data and many of the ideas in the text have been drawn. Also extremely useful was the catalogue for the exhibition organized at the Mosteiro dos Jerónimos by Anísio Franco, which revealed just how many treasures the monastery contains.

ALVES, Ana Maria, *Iconologia do Poder Real no Período Manuelino*, Lisbon I.N.-C M., 1985.

ALVES, José da Felicidade, *O Mosteiro dos Jerónimos*, vol. I, Lisbon, Horizonte, 1989.

ATANAZIO, M. C. Mendes, *A Arte do Manuelino*, Lisbon, Presença, 1984.

AVERINI, Ricardo, 'Sul Manuelino' in *Colóquio Artes*, 2nd series, no. 56, Mar. 1983.

BARREIRA, João, *Arte portuguesa. Evolução estética*, Lisbon, Excelsior, undated.

BARROS, João de, *Décadas da Ásia, I*, Coimbra, 1932.

BARROS, João de, *Panegíricos*, Lisbon, Sá da Costa, 2nd ed., 1943.

BARROS, João de, *Crónica do Imperador Clarimundo*, 2 vols., Lisbon, Sá da Costa, 1953.

BOOSCO DELEITOSO (1515 edition of the text with introduction, notes and glossary by Augusto Magne), Rio de Janeiro, Ministério da Educação e Saúde / Instituto Nacional do Livro, 1950.

BRANDI, Cesare, 'Il Manuelino' in *Struttura e Architettura*, Turin, Einaudi, 2nd ed. 1971, 301–307.

CHICÓ, Mario Tavares, 'A arquitectura em Portugal na época de D. Manuel e nos princípios do reinado de D. João III. O gótico final português, o estilo manuelino e a introdução da arte do renascimento' in *História da Arte em Portugal* (ed. Aarão de Lacerda), vol. II, Oporto, Portucalense Editora, 1948, 225–324.

CORREIA, Vergílio, *As obras de Santa Maria de Belém 1514 a 1519*, Lisbon, 1922.

CORREIA, Vergílio, *Monumentos e Esculturas*, Lisbon, 1924.

CORREIA, Vergílio, *A Arquitectura em Portugal no séc. XVI*, Sep. 'Biblos', vol. V, 1–2, Coimbra, Universidade de Coimbra, 1929.

CORREIA, Vergílio, 'Arte : ciclo manuelino' in *História de Portugal* (Barcelos), vol. IV, Portucalense Editora, 1933, 433–474.

DESWARTE, Sylvie, *Les Enluminures de la 'Leitura Nova' 1504–1522*, Paris, Fondation Calouste Gulbenkian, 1977.

DIAS, Pedro, 'A Arquitectura do Gótico final e a decoração Manuelina' in *O Manuelino* (vol. 5, da História de Arte em Portugal), Lisbon, Publicações Alfa, 1986, 7–91.

DIAS, Pedro, *A Arquitectura Manuelina*, Oporto, 1988.

DIAS, Pedro, *Os Portais Manuelinos do Mosteiro dos Jerónimos*, Coimbra, Universidade de Coimbra, 1993.

EVIN, Paul A., *Étude sur le style manuélin*, Paris, 1948.

EVIN, Paul A., 'Style manuelin et Spatgotik: les critiques du symbolisme maritime' in *Ciência e Trópico*, No. 2, vol. 13, 1985.

EVIN, Paul A., 'Faut-il voir un symbolisme maritime dans la decoration Manueline ?' in *Acte du Congrés International d'Histoire de l'Art*, vol. 2, 1949, 191–198.

FRANCO, Anísio (ed.), *Jerónimos. 4 Séculos de Pintura*, exhibition catalogue, Lisbon, IPPC, 1992.

GOIS, Damião de, *Crónica do Felicíssimo Rei D. Manuel*, 4 vols., Coimbra, Imp. da Univ., 1949–1954.

GOIS, Damião de, *Descrição da Cidade de Lisboa*, Lisbon, Horizonte, 1988.

KUBLER, George, *Portuguese Plain Architecture*, Middletown Wesleyan University Press, not dated.

LACERDA, Aarão de (ed.), *História da Arte em Portugal*, vol. I, Oporto, 1942.

LAMBERT, Élie, 'L'Art Manuelin', in *XVI Congrès d'Histoire de l'Art*, vol. I, Lisbon – Oporto, 1949, 13–20.

LEITE, Ana Cristina and Pereira, Paulo, 'Para uma leitura da simbólica manuelina' in *Prelo*, no. 5, Oct.–Dec. 1984, 51–74.

LEITE, Ana Cristina and PEREIRA, Paulo, 'São João verde, o Selvagem e o Gigante em Gil Vicente - apontamento iconológico' in *Estudos Portugueses. Homenagem a Luciana Stegagno Picchio*, Lisbon, Difel, 1991.

MARIAS, Fernando, *El Largo Siglo XVI*, Madrid, Taurus, 1989.

MARKl, Dagoberto, Baptista Pereira and Fernando António, *O Renascimento*, vol.6 of *História da Arte em Portugal*, Lisbon, Publicações Alfa, 1986.

MIGUEL, Fr. Jacinto de S., *Mosteiro de Belém*, Lisbon, 1901.

MOREIRA, Rafael, 'Arquitectura' in the Catalogue of the 17th Exhibition of Art, Science and Culture of the Council of Europe, Arte Antiga – I, Lisbon, 1983, 307–352.

MOREIRA, Rafael, *Jerónimos*, Lisbon, Verbo, 1987.

MOREIRA, Rafael, *A Arquitectura do Renascimento no Sul de Portugal*, Lisbon, 1991.

MOREIRA, Rafael, *A Arquitectura Militar na Expansão Portuguesa*, Oporto, CNCDP, 1994.

MOREIRA, Rafael, 'Santa Maria de Belém' in *O Livro de Lisboa*, Lisbon, Lisboa 94 / Horizonte, 1994.

MOREIRA, Rafael, 'A Torre de Belém' in *O Livro de Lisboa*, Lisbon, Lisboa 94 / Horizonte, 1994.

MUCHAGATO, Jorge and Saphieha, Nicolas, *Jerónimos. Memória e Lugar do Real Mosteiro*, Lisbon, Inapa, 1997.

PAIS DA SILVA, J. H, 'Rotas Artísticas no Reinado de D. Manuel I', *Panorama*, 4th series, 32, 1969.

PAIS DA SILVA, J. H, 'Manuelino' in *Enciclopédia Luso-Brasileira de Cultura*, vol. 12, Lisbon, ed. Verbo, 1971.

PEREIRA, Paulo and LEITE, Ana Cristina, 'Espiritualidade e religiosidade na Lisboa de Quinhentos' in *Lisboa Quinhentista*. Exhibition Catalogue, Lisbon, Câmara Municipal de Lisboa, 1983, 31–41.

Pereira, Paulo, *A Obra Silvestre e a Esfera do Rei*, Coimbra, Universidade de Coimbra, 1990.

PEREIRA, Paulo, 'L'architecture portugaise (1400–1550)' in *Feitorias*, exhibition catalogue from the exhibition (curator Pedro Dias), Antuérpia, Europália 91, 1991.

PEREIRA, Paulo, 'Retórica e Memória na simbologia manuelina. O caso de Santa Maria de Belém', *Lisboa, Jerónimos. 4 Séculos de Pintura* (ed. Anísio Franco), exhibition catalogue, Lisbon, IPPC, 1992a.

PEREIRA, Paulo, 'Gil Vicente e a contaminação das artes' in *Temas Vicentinos*. Proceedings from the Colloquium on the work of Gil Vicente, Lisbon, Diálogo, 1992.

PEREIRA, Paulo, 'A conjuntura artística e as mudanças de gosto' in *História de Portugal* (ed. José Mattoso), vol. III (ed. J. R. Magalhães), Lisbon, Círculo de Leitores, 1993.

PEREIRA, Paulo, 'Architecture manuéline: thèmes et problémes de méthode' in *A Travers l'Image*, Paris, Klinksieck / CNRS, 1993.

PEREIRA, Paulo, *Lisboa Manuelina*, Lisbon, IPM, 1994.

PEREIRA, Paulo, 'Iconografia dos Descobrimentos' in *Dicionário de História dos Descobrimentos*, vol. I, Lisbon, Círculo de Leitores, 1994.

QUADROS, António, *Introdução a uma estética existencial*, Lisbon, 1954.

QUINET, Edgar, *Mes vacances en Espagne*, Paris, Hachette, 1954.

SANSONETTI, Paul-Georges, 'Da Távola Redonda à Esfera Armilar : Ideal cavaleiresco e domínio do Mundo' in *Cavalaria Espiritual e Conquista do Mundo*, Lisbon, I.N.I.C., 1986, 43–48.

SANTOS, *Cândido dos, Os monges de S. Jerónimo em Portugal na Época do Renascimento*, I.C.L.P., Biblioteca Breve, 1984.

SANTOS, Reinaldo dos, *A Torre de Belém*, Coimbra, Imp. da Univ., 1922.

SANTOS, Reinaldo dos, 'O Mosteiro de Belém' in *A Arte em Portugal*, no. 10, Oporto, Marques Abreu, 1930.

SANTOS, Reinaldo dos, 'O Estilo Manuelino' in *Boletim da Academia Nacional de Belas Artes*, 1947.

SANTOS, Reinaldo dos, *O Estilo Manuelino*, Lisbon, 1952.

SANTOS, Reinaldo dos, *Oito séculos de Arte Portuguesa*, Lisbon, not dated.

SOUSA, Abade de Castro e, *Descripção do Real Mosteiro de Belém*, Lisbon, 2nd ed., 1840.

TELMO, António, *História Secreta de Portugal*, Lisbon, Guimarães, 1977.

TORRES, Fr. Alvaro de Torres, *Diálogo espiritual* (with an introduction by Candido dos Santos), Oporto, 1974.

VASCONCELOS, Joaquim de, *Da Architectura Manuelina*, Coimbra, 1885.

VIEIRA DA SILVA, José Custódio, *O tardo-gótico na arquitectura. A arquitectura religiosa do Alto Alentejo*, Lisbon, Horizonte, 1989.

VIEIRA DA SILVA, José Custódio, *Paço Medievais Portugueses. Caracterização e Evolução da Habitação Nobre. Séculos XII a XVI*, Lisbon, 1995.

INDEX